Small Sacrifice Huge Harvest

Small Sacrifice Huge Harvest

Simple Steps to Staying Afloat In An Ever-Changing Economy

Natalie Smith, MBA

AuthorHouse™
1663 Liberty Drive
Bloomington, IN 47403
www.authorhouse.com
Phone: 1-800-839-8640

© 2012 by Natalie Smith, MBA. All rights reserved.

No part of this book may be reproduced, stored in a retrieval system, or transmitted by any means without the written permission of the author.

Published by AuthorHouse   08/28/2012

ISBN: 978-1-4685-6031-2 (sc)
ISBN: 978-1-4685-6030-5 (e)

Library of Congress Control Number: 2012904118

Any people depicted in stock imagery provided by Thinkstock are models, and such images are being used for illustrative purposes only. Certain stock imagery © Thinkstock.

This book is printed on acid-free paper.

Because of the dynamic nature of the Internet, any web addresses or links contained in this book may have changed since publication and may no longer be valid. The views expressed in this work are solely those of the author and do not necessarily reflect the views of the publisher, and the publisher hereby disclaims any responsibility for them.

Contents

Chapter 1	The Most Common Gripe	1
Chapter 2	Money With A Mission	5
Chapter 3	Manipulating Your Money	9
Chapter 4	The 10-10-80 Plan	15
Chapter 5	Simple Financial Planning	33
Chapter 6	Escaping Foreclosure	39
Chapter 7	The Anatomy Of The Credit Report	49
Chapter 8	Money Saving Tips	59
Chapter 9	One of My Favorite Pass-Times	63

Glossary specific to Credit and Mortgage Terms............ 67

Professional Acknowledgements 119

Personal Acknowledgments 121

911, OUR FAMILY AND FRIENDS ARE IN CRISES. People within our own close-knit circle are in a state of financial distress and we are all oblivious to it because of the daily front that we practice so well. How is it that all we hear about in the media is how badly the economy is doing, how horrible the job market is, how much the foreclosure rate has risen within the recent years, how people are dying because they can't afford life insurance, but strangely, no one in our immediate circle appears to be suffering? The truth is that as proud people, we don't disclose these burdening facts with our friends and family. We are comfortable putting up the façade that everything is Peaches and Roses. Our society has created it so that if we're struggling financially that it's shameful. In some ways I can understand this line of thinking because as an American Society, we don't like to bring negative attention to our situation and we don't like being judged. Embarrassment is a hard feeling to live with, so rather than endure this shame and feeling of failure, we pretend it doesn't exist. As a result, we don't ask questions.

It's interesting that as children, we are taught that if we don't know something, we should ask a question and research until we find an answer. Unfortunately we don't practice what we preach. The sad part is that there is someone or something out there that can help each individual in every situation, but because of the shame we feel, we don't want to alert others that there's a problem, and that perhaps we could use some help. I agree with the saying "Information is key".

With this in mind, I always make it a point to share what I know with those in need of it. My disclaimer is "You can take what you need from it and do what you like with the rest". I am a great listener and have no problems allowing someone to vent, but if I am asked a question in an area in which I consider myself knowledgable, I feel it is my duty to at least offer information that may be beneficial to the next person.

In the last few years I've spoken with an uncountable number of people, all of whom needed help in certain areas but didn't know who to talk to or how to get the answers they needed. In my conversations I've found that many of them were grateful for the insight I passed on and actually applied certain formulas to their situations. Sometimes you don't realize the impact you have on someone until that person sincerely thanks you. There's nothing like a direct feeling of appreciation. I'm of course speaking from experience because I've been on the receiving end many times and I'm grateful that people have taken the time to educate me and offer suggestions. I heard someone say once, that if you find something that you are paid to do and you love it so much that would be willing to do for free, then you may have found your purpose. I am in constant search of my purpose in this life and I'm sure I'll continue to discover different levels of it, but I'll say this: "If this is my purpose for right now . . .

I'm okay with that". I am honored to share the following information with you in hopes that if you or someone you know is going through an overwhelming period in the area of finance, you can use this to your benefit or at the very least, pass it on to someone else.

I've created a self-help mini-guide for those who have occasional hardships from time to time. This book is designed to be used as a reference book for getting out of financial jams. I've divided it into three parts. Part one is a Financial Lecture. Part two Focuses on Foreclosure Prevention, and Part three focuses on Credit Scores. Along your read, you will find helpful tips that you should be able to use from day to day.

Chapter 1

The Most Common Gripe

I cannot begin to tell you how many times I've heard people say things like; "I can't keep living like this", "When am I going to make some real money?", "I have more going out than I have coming in", "I can't even afford a vacation after working so hard.", "It sure would be nice to treat myself to something nice, but I have bills to pay". And my all time favorite: "When tax time comes around I'll..."

Let's be honest about this thing; when tax time comes around chances are that we will be in a position to do **nothing**!! It's quite possible we'll be in the same situation we were in last year and the year before that. It's common for us to consume ourselves with debt, or increase our expenses (due to circumstances beyond our control) and then struggle through the rest of the year in hopes of getting a great tax refund from the government. Plans are often made way before we even file our income taxes. The problem with taxes is that too many people are in bondage to it. We create all these *"to do's"* in our minds with what we're going to do with this imaginary money, that by the time it gets to us, it's already spent. The bottom line is that the things on the infamous *"to do"* list are going to be decreased by 50% partly because not all of us are disciplined enough to make a plan and stick to it . . . which leads me to the purpose of this chapter.

Working for a well-known Non-Profit Agency, has allowed me to help others gain financial freedom through education. A misconception is that a person needs to make a substantial amount of money in order to live a comfortable debt free life. I must admit that once upon a time I thought the same way. We create our own stories about how different our lives would be "if only" we made X amount of money. The fact is that no matter how much money is placed into our hands, if we have no self-discipline, or management skills, it won't make a bit of difference. For example, Taxes are a big deal in our economy. A good majority of us mismanage money throughout the year and rely on our income tax refund to repair the damage. If we are disciplined with our earnings in the first place, then by the time the refund comes in, it can actually go to more positive things. I believe that if we've been educated in a particular subject area, we should be held accountable for it. It can never be said that we didn't know, because we've already been educated. Hence, we are responsible for the information given to us. It's the same in the case of a Parent and a Child. *If a 5-year-old jumps up and down on his parent's bed and the parent says nothing, chances are the 5 year old will continue to do it because he has not been corrected. He has no clue that it's a problem. Now if the parent scolds the child and explains that it is unacceptable to jump on the bed, at that point he will know that he shouldn't do it. Lets say that some time goes by and he decides to jump on the bed again; he knows by now that he's not to do it because he's been taught that it's unacceptable, but at that moment he chooses not to listen; he will now have to endure whatever the consequences are of jumping on the bed. Whether he falls and gets hurt, or he is firmly scolded by a parent, it is a lesson learned. The point is that he's been educated on one of the rules of the home. He is now held accountable for the information he's received. Just as children are held accountable for their actions, so are we as adults.* This leads me to sharing some vital information with you. Sometimes it gets overwhelming thinking about what you would do if some money came into your hands suddenly. For a lot of us, tax time would be a time to think about that. The next chapter will suggest some smart uses for your Tax Refund. By the way, if you are not ready to be held accountable, you should stop right here.

Chapter 2

Money With A Mission

Debt is a nasty word. As long as you're in debt to any person or creditor, you can't sincerely enjoy the money you've worked for. What you need to understand is that every dollar that comes into your hands has a direct mission; it's up to you to carry it out. The first thing you should want to do before you buy that new stereo, or set of golf clubs, or the fancy watch that you've been eyeing since *last tax season*, is to add up all your debt and start paying them off. Even if your Tax Return is barely enough to cover your debt you have to make an effort to get it lowered. **Pay Down On Your Credit Card Debt.** The faster you pay off your credit cards, the more money you save in interest payments. See which cards carry the highest interest rates and pay towards them first. Give your refund check a chance to save you money!

Put Money Towards Your Retirement. No matter how young you are, you need to start funding your retirement. Retirement is not something you start saving for WHEN YOU RETIRE. The earlier you place money into a savings plan, the longer it has to grow. Remember that a smart investment now could result in big money later. **<u>STOP</u>!!** If you don't have a retirement savings plan as of yet, it's never too *early* to start. A tax refund is an excellent source for your first contribution.

Protect Your Assets. A lot of folks think that once they've acquired certain assets then they've "arrived". To be honest, anyone can acquire an asset but not everyone can keep it. The key is nurturing and maintaining what you have. A neglected automobile can cost thousands to repair. Use your refund money to make sure that your car is up to par. It's called preventative maintenance. Don't wait until something goes wrong to check the engine. In addition, fixing the roof on your home, replacing the hot water heater, or updating the air conditioning unit will help to maintain your largest asset . . . 'your home'. Taking Preventative Measures like these could potentially save you larger expenses later.

Save For Certain Expenses. If your normal monthly expenses have not changed, put your refund aside for specific expenses such as holiday shopping, summer vacation, or even back-to-school costs. This way when these things come up, you don't have to get into the same cycle of putting it on credit and paying 5 times as much later, once you factor in the interest rate. You will be prepared if you save your refund check instead of spending it right away. Those extra expenses throughout the year may not be so stressful if you chose this route. You may view them differently now that you know you have the funds to cover them.

Create A Savings Cushion. This one can be a little more taxing to do. Setting aside 3 to 6 months of living expenses is always wise. You may not be able to predict the future, but you can set up a safety net of funds in the event something should pop up unexpectedly. There may be a medical emergency or some type of financial

Small Sacrifice, Huge Harvest

ordeal that may ordinarily throw you off-track. One very realistic example is the loss of a job. In many states across the Country, there is no such thing as Job Security. If the company's budget is looking slim one year, budget cuts are waiting around the corner for the next victim. This could very well be you. It's always a good idea to secure yourself with a nice savings to help you through the transition, should this situation arise.

Save For A Down Payment On A Home. If you don't already own a home, and intend to in the near future, it would be a great feeling to know that you have a nice down payment in the bank just waiting for you to qualify for a loan. It's not uncommon for people to pay the same amount in rent as others pay in mortgage each month. It seems that one of the obstacles that hold us back from purchasing a home is the down payment. Coming up with the monthly payment is easy for the most part, but down payments and closing costs are huge obstacles. Consider putting that money towards a great asset for yourself.

Pay An Extra Payment Towards Mortgage. If you already own a home, chances are you are paying a monthly mortgage payment. Well did you know that if you paid JUST ONE extra payment per year, you could reduce the term of your loan by several years? For example if you have a 30 year mortgage and you paid 13 payments as apposed to your normal 12 each year, you could shorten the life of your loan by 7 WHOLE YEARS!! Wouldn't it be great to know that you could be out of debt quicker than the expected time? Just think, you could take your refund and put it towards your house payment. In essence, all you would be doing is taking money from one account and putting it into another. As you may already know, each time you put money into your home, you're increasing your equity. ***Just be sure that any extra that you pay on your mortgage specifies that it should go directly to the principal!*** These are just some tips I wanted to share with you. Hopefully you've been able to chose at least one and commit to doing it. Since you've been educated, you are now accountable for the information that's been passed on to you. You can never again say those three little words where your Tax Return is concerned, *"(I **didn't know**)"*. Now before you continue I want to give you another opportunity to back out. Remember, you're still responsible for this information so if you're uninterested, you may want to stop here. Everyone else . . . may continue.

Chapter 3

Manipulating Your Money

It's easy to look at all the things we wish we had, and all the things we would do provided money was at our finger tips. For as much time as we spend daydreaming, the question is, do we ever think about how much debt we actually have? Do we know how to work with what we have to get the things we want? Well we first need to know these things before we start making any haste decisions, don't we? Lets' break it down! The realistic financial aspects of our lives are broken down into three areas. *The first area is Debt, the second area is Expenses, and the third area is Savings.* How we handle each of these areas is crucial to where we end up in life. First and foremost, let me share a **"public secret"** with you. If you find that living month to month is a financial struggle for you, you have to do one of two things. You need either to increase your income or decrease your expenses. First understand that *you* should manipulate your money, your money shouldn't manipulate *you*. After you have looked for areas where you can decrease your expenses, you then need to find ways to bring in more monthly income. One way to do that is to change your deductions in your paycheck. If you have less deducted now, you will obviously bring home more money. Don't get caught up in getting a big refund at tax time. If you reduce your deductions, your net increase will benefit you more if you discipline yourself to managing it better each month. What many of us don't realize is that the government borrows that money from us and earns interest on it throughout the year. Once they are done with it, we then get a **portion** of it back when we file our taxes. We get into this cycle of having **so much** deducted from our salary causing a shortage each month. Once there isn't enough cash on hand to take care of what we need or want, then credit cards and loans come into play. Often we find that something will come up that causes us to fall behind on our debts and expenses. This game of catch-up is what we play until our *Tax Refund* gets to us. We put so much emphasis on getting a big refund to take care of problems we got into during the previous year, when in actuality if we had access to that extra portion of our money each month, receiving such a large refund wouldn't seem as urgent. If you're receiving a few thousand dollars back each time you file and you don't have a lot of itemizations, perhaps you'd like to consider changing your deductions. If the *government* is benefiting from your labor, why shouldn't you? As long as you are reporting your income and being honest about your lifestyle you should have nothing to worry about. The last thing you need is an Audit. That's just a helpful tip for those of you who are looking for a few extra dollars per month.

Debt. It's important that you know who and what you owe. Keeping track of how much money you owe to your creditors will benefit you in the long run. If you were to walk up to someone randomly in the street and ask them off the top of their heads to tell you exactly what

Small Sacrifice, Huge Harvest

they owe, they probably wouldn't know. In our society we are so afraid of our debt that some of us don't even open our bills. Unfortunately, it's common to not address the issues we're unable to solve in a day. Intelligent financial decisions are based on accurate information. The area of debt is split into two categories. The first of the two is the **Almighty Credit Card**. My advice is to use credit only if you have to. You need to set up a plan that will allow you to pay off the balance in less than 6 months. Six months is pushing it but it's at least a short-term goal that will allow you to be in control of your debt. The longer you take to pay off your credit cards the greater the risk of you paying way more than you intended to for the product or service. Before you know it you'll be hit with late fees and over-the-limit fees, along with the interest rates. Another thing that gets us in trouble with these cards is the fact that we often don't know our rights. I find that **READING** is a missing element when it comes to this topic. Many of us don't read the fine print or even bother to read the inserts in the envelopes. Customers have the right to refuse an increase in interest rate and close the account. Many times they can refuse the new terms and pay off the balance at the pervious interest rate. Unfortunately the creditor knows that 9 out of 10 times we as consumers won't read this information and will continue to pay.

The second category is Loans. You must understand all terms of a loan when borrowing money. Do not allow yourself to be rushed into a decision and never sign anything until all your questions have been answered to your satisfaction. If you're feeling pressured or confused just walk away. Another key point is not to over-borrow. Just because you qualify for a huge mortgage, a line of credit, or a luxury car, it doesn't mean you should borrow that much money. Determine what payment fits your particular financial situation and make an intelligent decision.

Expenses. It's also important to live within our own means. The simplest way to avoid financial problems (**aside from unpredicted expenses**) is to spend less than we earn. It's wise to create a spending plan and stick to it. Expenses can easily get out of hand. Nip it in the bud before it gets beyond your control. Expenses are a result of your lifestyle. Re-evaluate your daily, weekly, and monthly activities. First, take a look at the necessary expenses like Shelter, Transportation, Utilities, Groceries, Insurance, Childcare . . . etc. then take a look at your variable expenses like Car Maintenance, Home Maintenance, Self Maintenance, Entertainment . . . etc. Determine how you can either cut back or develop a strategy for balancing everything out. Once you're able to get your debt out of the way, managing you're expenses should be less stressful. The key is *budget, budget, budget!!*

Savings. Unfortunately in a lot of cases, savings takes a back seat to expenses and debt because there's usually nothing left over. It's important to try and put aside something for emergencies. As stated earlier, 3 months of living expenses to avoid unwanted credit balances later is a great investment. If you should ever lose your job, you would have a small savings to use rather than adding to your debt load by using credit cards. Plan for the future. Set short and long-term financial goals and put yourself in charge of where your money goes. Remember we spoke about retirement earlier? And we'll touch on it again later. You won't want to work forever, and without a plan for your retirement years, you may have to work a lot longer than you'd like. As it is now, elder citizens can't afford to retire at 65 anymore because Social Security Income just isn't enough. Think about having to be responsible for a mortgage or a car note at that age with limited income. Social Security benefits can barely cover basic living expenses. In addition, I think that many of us take it for granted that by the time it's time for us to retire, this particular benefit will still be around. Just remember not every institution is as loyal as you may think. There comes a time when some things just stop with no explanation as to why. I do hope that as you read further you are enlightened and perhaps have started to ponder a bit on the things I'm sharing with you. Once again because I value my readers, I want to offer you another escape route just in case you can't handle the truth. You may opt to **STOP** here if you do not want to be accountable for this next set of information. If you're ready to make some life changing moves . . . be my guest!

Chapter 4

The 10-10-80 Plan

I'm glad you decided to read on. At the close of this section you will be required to take a challenge. Hopefully it will be to your benefit. We'll soon see, won't we?

Provided that there are no major changes, be it triumph or tragedy that takes place in your life on a monthly basis, the smartest way to live is below your means. In other words, the amount of money you bring in monthly should be more than what goes out. In this way, you always know that you can afford your lifestyle. There is a plan that is commonly referred to as **Ten-Ten-Eighty**. It is not well known to the point of everyday conversation but it has been referred to contextually as a means of Financial Planning. There is no set documentation as there would be with a 401K or a Mutual Fund Account, or any other type of official institution by which one would manage money. With this plan, instead of paying a financial planner to manage your money for you, it would be totally up to you to discipline yourself each pay period.

I was first introduced to this financial method in a pre-marital counseling session. We were told that it would be a good idea to Give Away 10% of our income, Save 10%, and Live Off 80%. The idea behind this was to encourage Selflessness and Discipline. And I have to say that it has worked for me. Okay, it goes as follows:

Charity would be the first part of the Plan to contribute to. Tithing is a very touchy subject in our society. I am not one to impose my views on others when it comes to this area but I will never down-play my feelings about it. Speaking from a Christian viewpoint, I firmly believe that nothing we have belongs to us. One hundred percent (100%) belongs to God. His only requirement where money is concerned is that we give the church the first 10% and he trusts us to manage the other 90%. If you ask me, I think that's getting off easy considering that if it weren't for Him (God) we'd have nothing. He afforded us the breath of life so that we could earn money to live, and instead of asking for it all, he takes the liberal approach and requires a mere 10%, which incidentally is less than what the Government will take from us (plus the Government takes its cut right off the top, no questions asked). I find it insane that people will honor the Government before honoring God (but that's another story isn't it?). Think about it! What if God were to make some immediate changes? What if he were to say, "I think I'm getting the short end of the stick! I think I'll start charging one cent per minute for the air I supply, that ought to cover the tithe!" Where would we be then? In bad shape I would imagine. We probably would be wishing we did the initial 10% in the first place, at least that way we'd still have 90% to play with, huh? Okay, well enough about that.

In actuality, 10% should go to Charity. It should be given away to an organization of your choice, perhaps even to someone less fortunate than you are, or to help a specific mission. Anything that allows you the opportunity to give of yourself would fall into this category. Once we get the revelation that it's *not always about us*, and the money that's placed into our hands is partially to help others, then we've freed ourselves from Selfishness and Greed. Remember that God rewards a cheerful giver so as we're giving out of our need with a clean heart, our reward is already on its way. Aside from knowing that it will come back to us, there's a feeling of gratitude that comes along with it. To know that we've helped someone else and that our money has a specific mission is a great reward in itself. My particular Charity just happens to be the Tithe to the Church. Think about what your Charity should be!

HERE ARE SOME SCRIPTURES THAT PERTAIN TO GIVING:

Deuteronomy 15:10 Give generously to him and do so without a grudging heart; then because of this the Lord your God will bless you in all your work, and in everything you put your hand to.

Deuteronomy 16:17 Every man shall give as he is able, according to the blessing of the LORD your God which He has given you.

1 Chronicles 29:9 Then the people rejoiced because they had offered so willingly, for they made their offering to the Lord with a whole heart, and King David also rejoiced greatly.

Proverbs 3:9-10 Honor the Lord from your wealth and from the first of all your produce; so your barns will be filled with plenty and your vats will overflow with new wine.

Proverbs 3:27 Do not withhold good from those to whom it is due, when it is in your power to do it.

Proverbs 11:24-25 There is one who scatters, and yet increases all the more, and there is one who withholds what is justly due, and yet it results only in want. The generous man will be prosperous, and he who waters will himself be watered.

Proverbs 21:26 . . .the righteous gives and does not hold back.

Proverbs 22:9 He who is generous will be blessed, for he gives some of his food to the poor.

Proverbs 28:27 He who gives to the poor will never want, but he who shuts his eyes will have many curses.

Malachi 3:10 "Bring the whole tithe into the storehouse, so that there may be food in My house, and test Me now in this," says the Lord of hosts, "if I will not open for you the windows of heaven and pour out for you a blessing until it overflows.

Matthew 6:3-4 But when you give to the poor, do not let your left hand know what your right hand is doing, so that your giving will be in secret; and your Father who sees what is done in secret will reward you.

Mark 12:41-44 And He sat down opposite the treasury, and began observing how the people were putting money into the treasury; and many rich people were putting in large sums. A poor widow came and put in two small copper coins, which amount to a cent. Calling His disciples to Him, He said to them, "Truly I say to you, this poor widow put in more than all the contributors to the treasury; for they all put in out of their surplus, but she, out of her poverty, put in all she owned, all she had to live on."

Luke 3:11 And he would answer and say to them, "The man who has two tunics is to share with him who has none; and he who has food is to do likewise."

Luke 6:30 Give to everyone who asks of you, and whoever takes away what is yours, do not demand it back.

Luke 6:38 Give, and it will be given to you. They will pour into your lap a good measure, pressed down, shaken together, and running over. For by your standard of measure it will be measured to you in return.

Acts 20:35 In everything I showed you that by working hard in this manner you must help the weak and remember the words of the Lord Jesus, that He Himself said, 'It is more blessed to give than to receive.

Romans 12:8 . . .Or he who exhorts, in his exhortation; he who gives, with liberality; he who leads, with diligence; he who shows mercy, with cheerfulness.

2 Corinthians 9:6-8 Now this I say, he who sows sparingly will also reap sparingly, and he who sows bountifully will also reap bountifully. Each one must do just as he has purposed in his heart, not grudgingly or under compulsion, for God loves a cheerful giver. And God is able to make all grace abound to you, so that always having all sufficiency in everything, you may have an abundance for every good deed.

2 Corinthians 9:10 Now He who supplies seed to the sower and bread for food will supply and multiply your seed for sowing and increase the harvest of your righteousness;

Philippians 4:15-17 And you yourselves also know, Philippians, that at the first preaching of the gospel, after I departed from Macedonia, no church shared with me in the matter of giving and receiving but you alone; for even in Thessalonica you send a gift more than once for my needs. Not that I seek the gift itself, but I seek for the profit which increases to your account.

James 2:15-16 If a brother or sister is without clothing and in need of daily food, and one of you says to them, "Go in peace, be warmed and be filled," and yet you do not give them what is necessary for their body, what use is that?

Choose one that speaks to you and use it to encourage you each time you're tempted not to give. I decided to go with Mark 12:41-44 myself. Whenever I find myself trying to justify why I don't need to give, this particular scripture helps me to get back on track. I'm not in the business of missing out on any blessings.

Some common phrases I hear are, "I can't afford to save, I can't afford to give, I can barely afford to take care of myself". Sound familiar? And no I don't read minds? I just happen to have the same conversation over and over again with different people. I can probably relate to these phrases more than anyone else because I myself

Small Sacrifice, Huge Harvest

have experienced what it's like to earn low wages, have high bills, and have little for myself. I use to practice what I call the Ten-Ninety Plan, which is where I would tithe 10% and struggle with my 90%. I felt that as long as I was taking care of God's business with that first 10%, then he didn't care what I did with the remaining 90%. The 90% was for me to do what ever I wanted. But I noticed that although tithing would keep me afloat, it wasn't really affording me the opportunity to do even the little things. For example, I never traveled because I didn't have any money. I never got my hair done because I couldn't spare it, I wouldn't even go into the malls because I assumed there was nothing in there I could afford. I felt like I had no business shopping or getting nice things for myself because I already had the luxury of having my own place and my own car. I had acquired this style of living and it was my responsibility to pay my bills with room for nothing else. Nothing was put aside for the future.

This brings me to the second 10% of the plan. **Savings** is a big deal in our society; in fact, it's more accepted than charity. It's actually encouraged to the point where the Government will take Social Security Income out of our checks to secure at least a few dollars for retirement. Now of course history has proven that Social Security Income can't realistically afford us a decent life; this is why there are opportunities for us to save towards retirement. We have 401K's available, Annuities, Stocks, Personal Retirement Funds, Savings Accounts, and the list goes on.

One day in all of my confusion regarding my finances, God literally pulled me to the side and said, "*Do you trust me?*" I responded in my mind, "Sure, that's why I tithe; I know you'll take care of me". He then said, "*Well why is it taking you so long to do the things that I tell you to do?*"

Of course I was clueless, because as far as I knew I had been doing my part with his 10%. "I don't understand," I said. He then said, *"You've taken care of the tithe, but what about paying yourself? Don't you think I want you to be comfortable? Don't you think that I want you to secure yourself?"* WOW! Please bear in mind that at this point I was clearly talking to myself. Anyone passing by would have thought I was nuts. It didn't occur to me that I was actually having a conversation with God until weeks later when it hit me. He said, *"I know that you don't have much to spare and don't you worry I'll take care of that real soon, but **AT THE VERY LEAST** you need to start paying yourself what you tithe to me"*. It never dawned on me that I should do that. Instead of living off the 90%, I could take the same amount that I tithe, and create a savings for myself. I've always been conservative when it came to investing and risk-taking, so of course at the time I chose the safest route I knew, and opted to take an additional 10% of my income and put it into a savings account. Soon after, I started contributing to a 401K along with some other private funds. After all, it was only 10% and I still had 80% left to live from, which now brings me to the final part of the plan.

HERE ARE SOME SCRIPTURES THAT PERTAIN TO SAVING:

Genesis 41:34-36 Let Pharaoh take action to appoint overseers in charge of the land, and let him exact a fifth of the produce of the land of Egypt in the seven years of abundance. "Then let them gather all the food of these good years that are coming, and store up the grain for food in the cities under Pharaoh's authority, and let them guard it. "Let the food become as a reserve for the land for the seven years of famine, which will occur in the land of Egypt, so that the land will not perish during the famine.

Proverbs 6:6-8 Go to the ant, o sluggard, observe her ways and be wise, which, having no chief, officer or ruler, prepares her food in the summer and gathers her provision in the harvest.

Proverbs 13:16 A wise man thinks ahead; a fool doesn't, and even brags about it!

Proverbs 13:19 Desire realized is sweet to the soul, but it is an abomination to fools to turn away from evil.

Proverbs 15:22 Without consultation, plans are frustrated, but with many counselors they succeed.

Proverbs 16:1 The plans of the heart belong to man, but the answer of the tongue is from the Lord.

Proverbs 20:18 Prepare plans by consultation, and make war by wise guidance.

Proverbs 21:5 The plans of the diligent lead surely to advantage, but everyone who is hasty comes surely to poverty.

Proverbs 22:3 The prudent sees the evil and hides himself, but the naive go on, and are punished for it.

Proverbs 24:3-4 By wisdom a house is built, and by understanding it is established; and by knowledge the rooms are filled with all precious and pleasant riches.

Proverbs 27:12 A prudent man sees evil and hides himself, the naive proceed and pay the penalty.

Proverbs 27:23 Know well the condition of your flocks, and pay attention to your herds;

Ecclesiastes 11:2 Divide your portion to seven, or even to eight, for you do not know what misfortune may occur on the earth.

Matthew 25:1-13 "Then the kingdom of heaven will be comparable to ten virgins, who took their lamps and went out to meet the bridegroom. Five of them were foolish, and five were prudent. For when the foolish took their lamps, they took no oil with them, but the prudent took oil in flasks along with their lamps. Now while the bridegroom was delaying, they all got drowsy and began to sleep. But at midnight there was a shout, 'Behold, the bridegroom! Come out to meet him.' Then all those virgins rose and trimmed their lamps. The foolish said to the prudent, 'Give us some of your oil, for our lamps are going out.' But the prudent answered, 'No, there will not be enough for us and you too; go instead to the dealers and buy some for yourselves.' And while they were going away to make the purchase, the bridegroom came, and those who were ready went in with him to the wedding feast; and the door was shut. Later the other virgins also came, saying, 'Lord, lord, open up for us.' But he answered, 'Truly I say to you, I do not know you.' Be on the alert then, for you do not know the day nor the hour."

Luke 12:16-21 And He told them a parable, saying, "The land of a rich man was very productive. And he began reasoning to himself, saying, 'What shall I do, since I have no place to store my crops?' Then he said, 'This is what I will do: I will tear down my barns and build larger ones, and there I will store all my grain and my goods. And I will say to my soul, "Soul, you have many goods laid up for many years to come; take your ease, eat, drink and be merry."' But God said to him, 'You fool! This very night your soul is required of you; and now who will own what you have prepared?' So is the man who stores up treasure for himself, and is not rich toward God."

Luke 14:28-30 For which one of you, when he wants to build a tower, does not first sit down and calculate the cost to see if he has enough to complete it? "Otherwise, when he has laid a foundation and is not able to finish, all who observe it begin to ridicule him, saying, 'This man began to build and was not able to finish.'"

1 Corinthians 16:1-2 Now concerning the collection for the saints, as I directed the churches of Galatia, so do you also. On the first day of every week each one of you is to put aside and save, as he may prosper, so that no collections be made when I come.

1 Timothy 6:7 For we have brought nothing into the world, so we cannot take anything out of it either.

Proverbs 21:5 The plans of the diligent lead surely to advantage, but everyone who is hasty comes surely to poverty.

Proverbs 21:20 There is precious treasure and oil in the dwelling of the wise, but a foolish man swallows it up.

Proverbs 27:12 A prudent man sees evil and hides himself, the naive proceed and pay the penalty

Proverbs 30:24-25 Four things are small on the earth, but they are exceedingly wise: The ants are not a strong people, but they prepare their food in the summer;

1 Corinthians 16:2 On the first day of every week each one of you is to put aside and save, as he may prosper, so that no collections be made when I come.

The most important element to working with what you have is management. Through my experience, I've found that many people are in such bondage to money, partly because they have no money managing skills. There is a popular phrase that says, "the more money you have the more problems come with it". Unfortunately, in many cases this is true but it doesn't necessarily have to be like that. Excluding the obvious obstacles like job loss, hospitalization, and other obstacles that you can't prepare for, provided that all factors remain the same, the key to money management is discipline. If you can discipline yourself to live off 80% of your income, then in fact you are living below your means. I've found that a lot of time has been wasted meditating on the things we don't have as apposed to the things we do have. It's easy to get caught

Small Sacrifice, Huge Harvest

up in what everyone else has. This is what hurts us the most when it comes to money. When we decide that we just have to have certain things it eventually leads to high expenses, which can ultimately turn into debt. The fact of the matter is; *the list of things we need is shorter than the list of things we want.* Debt is a lot of times an unnecessary burden in our society. In a society so rich with resources, it makes no sense for us to fuel the economy by placing ourselves into so much debt that we can't even sleep at night. Just as bad parents set horrible examples for their children, the Government has set a bad example for us in the area of finance. We are at times *Victims of our own Nation*. The United States Government is over Trillions of dollars in Debt to other Nations. Hence the reason for all the different taxes that we pay in so many areas. Along with that, the money has to come from somewhere and one convenient way to get it from the citizens is to make loans and establish credit. Credit Cards are what I believe to be one of the great demises of our society. The main reason why it is so difficult for most of us to get from under our credit card debt is because **SOCIETY IS DESIGNED TO KEEP US IN DEBT**. How else will the economy function if it's not earning money from interest rates, and late fees, and over the limit fees, and so forth? It keeps everyone in business. It is said, "Money Makes the World Go Around". The phrase really should state, "Debt Makes the World Go Around". Many do not realize the seriousness of it because it isn't presented in such a crucial manner. The media makes it seem normal. Once it's perceived as normal, it downplays the urgency to discipline ourselves. If a child has watched his parent live a certain way with no attempt to correct the situation, what example has that parent set for his child? It may not be perceived as wrong in his eyes because he looks up to his parent. Well it's the same with the Government and its Citizens. The Government is in debt to other countries, and this is the example that we've seen all of our lives. So if we're in debt to a few creditors, it's not that big of a deal in comparison to what the Government owes. The bottom line is if we're in debt as a Nation, it only seems logical that we have personal debt as citizens as well. Right? Wrong! When you convince yourself that 80% is all you have to work with, you'll think twice about the purchases you make, you'll hesitate before opening another credit card, you'll reevaluate how many bills you can really afford monthly, and this will help you manage what little you have. Instead of hoping and praying for more money to come into your hands, you'll start to appreciate what you do have, and work within your means. Once you're able to manage your current financial status successfully, you will eventually be blessed with a greater status to handle. The point is, if you can't manage $100, why should you be trusted with $1,000. In my opinion that's just more to mismanage.

HERE ARE SOME SCRIPTURES PERTAINING TO BUDGETING AND MONEY MANAGEMENT:

Proverbs 6:6-8 Go to the ant, sluggard; consider her ways and be wise; who having no guide, overseer, or ruler, provides her food in the summer and gathers her food in the harvest.

Proverbs 21:5 The thoughts of the diligent tend only to plenty; but the thoughts of everyone who is hasty only to poverty.

Proverbs 22:3 A prudent one foresees the evil and hides himself, but the simple pass on and are punished.

Proverbs 24:3-4 Through wisdom a house is built, and by understanding it is established; and by knowledge the rooms shall be filled with all precious and pleasant riches.

Proverbs 25:28 He who has no rule over his own spirit is like a broken down city without a wall.

Proverbs 27:12 A prudent man sees evil and hides himself, the naive proceed and pay the penalty.

Proverbs 27:23 Know well the face of your flocks; and pay attention to your herds.

Proverbs 27:26 The lambs are for your clothing, and the goats are the price of the field.

Luke 14:28-30 For which of you, intending to build a tower, does not sit down first and count the cost, whether he may have enough to finish it; lest perhaps, after he has laid the foundation and is not able to finish, all those seeing begin to mock him, saying, This man began to build and was not able to finish.

1 Corinthians 16:2 On the first day of every week each one of you is to put aside and save, as he may prosper, so that no collections be made when I come.

Proverbs 16:8 Better is a little with righteousness than great income with injustice.

Luke 16:10 He who is faithful in a very little thing is faithful also in much; and he who is unrighteous in a very little thing is unrighteous also in much.

Psalm 37:25 I have been young and now I am old, yet I have not seen the righteous forsaken or his descendants begging bread.

Matthew 6:31-32 Do not worry then, saying, 'What will we eat?' or 'What will we drink?' or 'What will we wear for clothing?' For the Gentiles eagerly seek all these things; for your heavenly Father knows that you need all these things.

Matthew 7:11 If you then, being evil, know how to give good gifts to your children, how much more will your Father who is in heaven give what is good to those who ask Him!

2 Corinthians 9:8 And God is able to make all grace abound to you, so that always having all sufficiency in everything; you may have an abundance for every good deed;

Philippians 4:19 And my God will supply all your needs according to His riches in glory in Christ Jesus.

1 Cor 16:2 "On the first day of every week each one of you is to put aside and save, as he may prosper, so that no collections be made when I come."

3 John 1:2 Beloved, I pray that you may prosper in all things and be in health, just as your soul prospers.

Small Sacrifice, Huge Harvest

Luke 12:42-44 And the Lord said, "Who then is the faithful and sensible steward, whom his master will put in charge of his servants, to give them their rations at the proper time? "Blessed is that slave whom his master finds so doing when he comes. "Truly I say to you that he will put him in charge of all his possessions.

Luke 12:47-48 And that slave who knew his master's will and did not get ready or act in accord with his will, will receive many lashes, but the one who did not know it, and committed deeds worthy of a flogging, will receive but few. From everyone who has been given much, much will be required; and to whom they entrusted much, of him they will ask all the more.

Luke 16:9-11 And I say to you, make friends for yourselves by means of the wealth of unrighteousness, so that when it fails, they will receive you into the eternal dwellings. "He who is faithful in a very little thing is faithful also in much; and he who is unrighteous in a very little thing is unrighteous also in much. Therefore if you have not been faithful in the use of unrighteous wealth, who will entrust the true riches to you?

Romans 14:8 For if we live, we live for the Lord, or if we die, we die for the Lord; therefore whether we live or die, we are the Lord's.

Deuteronomy 30:9 The Lord your God will then make you successful in everything you do. He will give you many children and numerous livestock, and he will cause your fields to produce abundant harvests, for the Lord will again delight in being good to you as he was to your ancestors.

Proverbs 22:4 The reward of humility and the fear of the Lord are riches, honor and life.

Chapter 5

Simple Financial Planning

Practicing this Plan will change your relationship with money. If you decide to try this out for 6 months you will not only see the difference, but you will also feel it. In essence, what you would be doing is **giving away 10%.** This will take care of that *poverty-minded-spirit*. It's common for us to not want to let go of anything because we never know if we'll get it back. We sometimes feel like we don't have enough to share, and this is the wrong attitude to have. The fact is, there is always someone financially worst off than we are. There will always be someone in need. There's a mission out there with each of our names on it that only our specific offering can cure. This is an opportunity to be obedient and stop hoarding what doesn't belong to you in the first place. Trust me, it's a weight lifted.

Paying yourself 10% is your reward for doing what's right. You work hard, and physically you should be able to reap the benefits of your labor. You owe it to you! Once you've given of yourself freely, the guilt that you may have from spending or vacationing while there are people without food, goes away because you know that at the very least you've done your part. The key is to limit your-self in the beginning. Put something aside for the future like retirement or for a rainy day. Also squeeze out something extra and treat yourself to something nice within reason. Sometimes there's no greater joy than pampering yourself with your own money. Not having to look for a handout, or borrow from someone is a great feeling. If you already have this money put aside, then you won't have to stress yourself out about where to find it when you need it. You'll already know because it will be untouched funds. That alone can put a smile on your face.

Living off 80% of your income sounds very difficult and maybe at first, but once you've conditioned yourself to something, it eventually gets easy, sort of like exercising. The Key to this part of the equation as stated earlier is **Managemen**t. You have to manage this money as though it were your own company. You need to tell yourself that you have to account for every dime. Tell yourself that it's unacceptable to put $50 in miscellaneous, just because you can't account for it. Once you learn to be detailed with your finances it will force you to change your attitude regarding money. The greatest thing about this Plan is that you can gradually work your way up to a comfortable percentage that works for you. You can start with lower numbers like Five-Five-Ninety (5%-5%-90%) or even lower if you need to.

The goal is to change your relationship with money, and discipline yourself to managing what you have now. This will help you to position yourself for bigger assets. Pretty soon you'll find out that you actually have a little extra left over to pay things off and get out of debt. Soon after that you may even be motivated enough to encourage others to do the same. Remember that the last thing God wants for us is to be in bondage to money, and consumed by debt. "Above all things the Lord wants us to be Prosperous and in Good Health". As I close this section this will be my prayer for you. Will you accept the challenge?

HERE ARE SOME SCRIPTURES PERTAINING TO CONTENTMENT:

Matthew 19:21-26 Jesus said to him, "If you wish to be complete, go and sell your possessions and give to the poor, and you will have treasure in heaven; and come, follow Me." But when the young man heard this statement, he went away grieving; for he was one who owned much property. And Jesus said to His disciples, "Truly I say to you, it is hard for a rich man to enter the kingdom of heaven. "Again I say to you, it is easier for a camel to go through the eye of a needle, than for a rich man to enter the kingdom of God." When the disciples heard this, they were very astonished and said, "Then who can be saved?" And looking at them Jesus said to them, "With people this is impossible, but with God all things are possible."

Mark 4:19 But the worries of the world, and the deceitfulness of riches, and the desires for other things enter in and choke the word, and it becomes unfruitful.

Mark 8:36 For what does it profit a man to gain the whole world, and forfeit his soul?

Matthew 6:31-33 "Do not worry then, saying, 'What will we eat?' or 'What will we drink?' or 'What will we wear for clothing?' "For the Gentiles eagerly seek all these things; for your heavenly Father knows that you need all these things.

"But seek first His kingdom and His righteousness, and all these things will be added to you.

Luke 3:14 Some soldiers were questioning him, saying, "And what about us, what shall we do?" And he said to them, "Do not take money from anyone by force, or accuse anyone falsely, and be content with your wages."

Philippians 4:11-13 For I have learned to be content, whatever the circumstances may be. I know now how to live when things are difficult and I know how to live when things are prosperous. In general and in particular I have learned the secret of eating well or going hungry of facing either plenty of poverty. I am ready for anything through the strength of the One who lives within me.

Hebrews 13:5 Keep your life free from the love of money, and be content with what you have.

James 4:1-3 What is the source of quarrels and conflicts among you? Is not the source your pleasures that wage war in your members? You lust and do not have; so you commit murder. You are envious and cannot obtain; so you fight and quarrel. You do not have because you do not ask. You ask and do not receive, because you ask with wrong motives, so that you may spend it on your pleasures.

Deuteronomy 15:6 For the Lord your God will bless you as He has promised you, and you will lend to many nations, but you will not borrow; and you will rule over many nations, but they will not rule over you.

Small Sacrifice, Huge Harvest

Deuteronomy 28:12 The Lord will open for you His good storehouse, 'the heavens, to give rain to your land in its season and to bless all the work of your hand; and you shall lend to many nations, but you shall not borrow.

2 Kings 4:7 Then she came and told the man of God. And he said, "Go, sell the oil and pay your debt, and you and your sons can live on the rest."

Psalm 37:21 The wicked borrows and does not pay back, but the righteous is gracious and gives.

Proverbs 22:7 The rich rules over the poor, and the borrower becomes the lender's slave.

Proverbs 22:26-27 Do not be a man who strikes hands in pledge or puts up security for debts; if you lack the means to pay, your very bed will be snatched from under you.

Ecclesiastes 5:5 It is better that you should not vow than that you should vow and not pay.

Romans 13:8 Owe nothing to anyone except to love one another; for he who loves his neighbor has fulfilled the law.

Proverbs 19:2 Also it is not good for a person to be without knowledge, and he who hurries his footsteps errs.

Chapter 6

Escaping Foreclosure

For some people, losing a home can feel like losing a loved one. The saddest thing is finding out later that it could have been prevented had we had access to the right kind of information. I have seen many people lose their homes due to lack of information. My heart breaks every time I think about all of the options they had available to them and didn't know it. I have made it my personal mission to get this information out to the public by any means necessary. It is a selfish act to hoard information that could in turn help someone else. I cannot in good conscience know the things that I know and only share it with those who come to me first. There are many who will never have the opportunity to encounter someone who can help them, so my goal is to make this information easily accessible to the general public.

My advice to homeowners is to keep this as a general guide to preventing foreclosure, as you may never know what the future holds for you. I also challenge you to do the right thing and purchase this guide for your family and neighbors that may own homes as well. In a time where inflation is consistently rising and the economy is fluctuating you never can tell what your situation will be in the next year. Facing foreclosure is very scary. It's also personal and in some cases embarrassing to the person that's going through it. Most times a homeowner will feel uncomfortable talking about it to friends or family for fear of being judged. It's because of this shame that foreclosure ultimately happens in a lot of cases. They don't know where to go, they're afraid to ask for monetary help, and they have no clue that there are programs that can help. Having a mini guide such as this for "just-in-case-scenarios" could make a world of difference in someone's life.

My hope is that once you've read all of the options available to saving your home, that you will feel it necessary to share this information with all homeowners whether they're in danger or not. You just never know!

Depending on the type of loan you have, your Lender may be able to offer different options to help you prevent foreclosure on your home. What many people don't know, is that there is a specific department designated to working with delinquent mortgage cases once they reach a certain amount of months behind. Once (you) the Borrower calls the lender in reference to a delinquent loan, the call is already flagged and then the screening process begins. The account continues to move from department to department depending on the severity of the default (for example, 2 months, 3 months ... etc).

The department that specifically handles loans before it goes to foreclosure is called the **Loss Mitigation Department**. To be quite honest, this is the only department that makes the decisions on whether or not to work with a Borrower, not Customer service, and definitely not Collections.

The first thing a Borrower must know is what type of loan he or she has. Loans are first classified as

Conventional, FHA (Federal Housing Administration), OR **VA (Veterans Administration).** Once that is determined, the Lender will do further research to find out the terms of the loan contract. Upon discovering this information, it makes it a little easier to decide what options are available to the Borrower. It sounds simple but it's quite tricky. Because Lenders don't want Borrowers abusing the available programs, they're required by The Department of Housing and Urban Development to start by offering the stricter options first, and gradually move to the more favorable options. They feel that if borrowers are made to work hard to prevent foreclosure, then the likelihood of the situation happening again would be few are far between. That being said, you'll begin to understand why, the options seem to become more ideal as the situation becomes increasingly worse.

The most common of the options begin with a **General Repayment Plan.** This is when the Customer Service Representative suggests that you send in a regular payment in addition to an extra one or two months until you're all caught up. This option in most cases is pretty unrealistic because the fact remains that if you had that type of money to begin with, perhaps you wouldn't be behind in the first place.

Remembering that the options must be offered in sequential order, the next option is called a **Forbearance Agreement.** In an agreement such as this, the mortgage company (lender) and the borrower (you) enter an agreement which states that they will take the delinquent balance and spread it out over 3 or 4 payments. You will then be required to pay your regular payment in addition to ½ or 1/3 of your regular mortgage payment. As you can calculate, the monthly payment will be higher for a few months until the delinquent balance is paid off. Once the debt is settled, the payments go back to normal and everything is on track. It is very important that this agreement is not broken, because it's actually more binding than the initial agreement in most cases. Depending on the state you live in, failure to comply with the terms of a Forbearance Agreement can result in immediate action to foreclose.

The next option, which is a pretty difficult one to get is called a **Special Forbearance Agreement**. With this option, the lender can lower the mortgage payment by up to **50%** for several months and then once that period is up, the borrower may be required to pay **150%** of his or her payment for the next several months. For example, if the normal payment is $1000, in order to give the borrower time to come up with the money, they may decrease the payment to $500 for 6 months. The downside is that once the break ends, the borrower may be required to pay $1500 for the following six months to incorporate the $1000 + the initial $500. This option is only available on **FHA** loans.

The next option is called a **Modification**. This plan can work two ways. The **first type** of Modification is when the Lender takes the entire delinquent balance and spreads it out throughout the remaining life of the loan, causing the regular mortgage payment to go up slightly. This new payment will be permanent. For example if the delinquent balance is $4000 and the Borrower has 20 years (basically 240 months) left to pay off the loan, the Lender would then divide $4000 by 240 months to come up with $16.70. This amount represents how much the new monthly payment would increase. So if the normal payment is usually $1000, then the new payment would be $1016.70 for the remaining life of the loan. With this method, the borrower is paying a minimal payment each month to take care of the delinquent balance, and the mortgage payment is now considered up to date.

The **second type** of modification works a little like a refinance. The Lender will in some cases lower the interest rate or extend the term of the loan to help the borrower. If the interest rate is more than 2% above market rate the Lender can refinance the remaining term at a lower rate causing the payment to decrease slightly. Of course the delinquent balance is added into the new term, but the interest rate will be lower. On the same note, the lender may decide to extend the loan by a few years, which may also cause the payment to decrease.

Another Option that not too many people know about is called a **VA Refunding**. This plan is only available on VA loans. This is when VA will purchase the loan from the Lender and refinance it for the Borrower. In some cases it may result in a lower interest rate. This frees the Borrower from the current Lender and erases the debt. The new loan will then be paid directly the the Veterans Administration. There are very strict guidelines for this option.

The final option is called a **Partial Claim**. This plan like the Special Forbearance Agreement is very difficult to get and is also only available on **FHA** loans. This is when FHA steps in and pays off the delinquent balance for the Borrower. Once the balance is paid and the mortgage is brought up to date, FHA will then place a silent lien on the house. The payment of the delinquent balance is due in full to FHA once the mortgage is paid off. The Borrower continues to make regular mortgage payments each month to the Lender until the term has ended. Immediately after the final mortgage payment, FHA expects to be paid. This is also the case if the house is sold, or the loan is refinanced. The down side to this option is that partial payments are not accepted, it must be a one time payment. The up side is, this loan is interest free. If the loan is for $4000 today, then 20 years later, the borrower will still owe $4000.

In the case of a conventional loan, some borrowers may be paying something called **PMI**, which is short for **Private Mortgage insurance.** Private Mortgage Insurance is an institution that insures the mortgage company in the event that the homeowner stops making payments. In some cases, the homeowner can contact the PMI company directly and ask for help. It actually saves the PMI from taking such a huge loss should the lender foreclose on the home. The PMI company may actually make a small loan to the Homeowner with a low interest rate to help them bring the mortgage current.

As we all know, not everyone is in a position to keep their home, no matter how badly they want to stay. In this type of situation, the Borrower can opt to do a **Pre-Foreclosure Sale**, also known as a **Short Sale**. This is when the bank will allow the Borrower some time to sell the home before the bank takes it. In this case the Bank will often accept less than the total loan amount and forgive the borrower for the difference. It's important to understand that the amount forgiven by the bank must be reported when filing taxes because the borrower will be expected to pay taxes on it. There are guidelines that apply just as with the previous options, so be sure to request an application. This option requires either a Real Estate Agent that is knowledgeable in Pre-foreclosure Sales, or an Experienced Investor. Be very careful when choosing an Investor. There are a lot of Predators out there.

As a last resort, if the home is unable to be sold for any reason, the Lender may agree to take back the deed from the borrower and cancel the remaining debt. This option is called A **Deed In Lieu Of Foreclosure.** The upside is that the Borrower walks away from whatever is owed and avoids foreclosure. The downside is that the Borrower also walks away from the equity he or she has in the home as well. Also, although foreclosure is prevented, The Deed in Lieu can still be reflected on the Credit Report. Be sure to talk to a tax advisor regarding tax obligations in this situation.

Below is an example of a Hardship letter. This is one of the first things your mortgage company will ask for. The company wants to know exactly why you've fallen behind and if you have a plan to fix it. Just a heads up, some of the programs available will deny you, if you repeatedly have the same reason for falling behind in the past. If there happen to be a number of reasons that you fell behind, try to list the most crucial one. It doesn't do you any good to give them the laundry list of woes when it won't help you, and could possibly even hurt you, should it happen again in the near future. At that point, you're considered a repeat offender. As much as you're advised to contact the mortgage company right away if you're experiencing problems, the truth is, they're only interested in how your going to fix the situation. Keep your sob stories simple, and ask them for the program that would work best for you. Find out what you're eligible for and keep it moving.

Natalie Smith, MBA

Hardship Example Letter:

To Whom it May Concern:

I am writing this letter to explain my late payments on my mortgage loan #12345 to XYZ Mortgage Company, starting in February 2010.

I am very distressed that this has ever happened to me, but I was <laid off>, <seriously injured>, <going through a death in family>. The circumstances drained my savings and I was forced to miss multiple payments because of it. I have sought financial counseling from an approved counseling agency for guidance in keeping my home.

I would like to apply for some type of Loan Modification that would adjust my payments to something more affordable for my situation. I am currently looking for ways to earn more income, but in the meantime I do not want to lose my home. I will be happy to provide any documents you may need during this process if you feel there is a program that can help me to get back on track with my payments and avoid foreclosure. I thank you in advance for your time and immediate response to this letter.

Sincerely,
Your Signature

Small Sacrifice, Huge Harvest

HERE IS AN EXAMPLE OF A BUDGET FORM (COMMONLY REFERRED TO AS A WORKSHEET) THAT THE MORTGAGE COMPANY MIGHT HAVE YOU FILL OUT, IN ORDER TO DETERMINE WHICH PROGRAM YOU QUALIFY FOR.

Monthly Budget	
Income - After Tax	Amount
Income #1	
Income #2	
Other	
Total Income	
Expenses	Amount
Tithe	
Savings	
Housing - Mortgage/Rent	
Electric	
Gas	
Water	
Phone	
Cable	
Sewer	
Trash	
Internet	
Food	
Credit Card Payment #1	
Credit Card Payment #2	
Credit Card Payment #3	
Credit Card Payment #4	

Loan Payment	
Car Payment #1	
Car Payment #2	
Auto Repairs and Tags	
Auto Gas	
Auto Insurance	
General Merchandise (Non-Food)	
Clothes	
Haircuts	
Gifts - Birthdays and Holidays	
Social and Entertainment	
Other	
Other	
Other	
Other	
Other	
Total Expenses	

Of course for every option, there are specific requirements. Unfortunately the Lenders don't usually disclose this information with the public. It's difficult to know what to say, whom to ask for, what to show, and things of that nature. This is why it's important to speak with someone knowledgeable, such as a **Certified Housing Counselor** who can assess your situation and guide you through the process before speaking with the Mortgage Company. This way you can be fully prepared when speaking with the Lender and the transition will be a lot smoother because you'll have a better understanding of the procedures.

Chapter 7

The Anatomy Of The Credit Report

*General Tips for Understanding and
Improving Your Credit Score*

A solid credit score plays a tremendous role in helping you secure the best rates on mortgages, automobile loans, credit cards, personal lines of credit, and more. Consumers with lower credit scores will be less likely to get approval for zero interest rate promotions or take advantage of opportunities to transfer balances to credit lines with lower interest rates. Knowing what makes up your credit score, should be part of an overall strategy to maintain your financial health.

According to a reoccurring study done by the **Consumer Federation of America**, a consumer with an average credit score of 700 would reduce finance charges by $76 each year by increasing his score 30 points. "A credit score is a vital component of overall credit health, Lenders use credit scores to measure the care that consumers take with their credit and to determine the likelihood that they will repay money borrowed."

Natalie Smith, MBA

Everyone wants to know "What makes up a credit score"?

A credit score is a rating based ONLY on information found in your credit report, such as previous credit performance, how much debt you currently have, how long you have had established credit accounts, and the types of credit available to you. A credit score is NOT based on factors such as race, gender, color, religion, national origin, and marital status. Additionally, your income, employment, and residence are not part of your credit score. The most common credit score used in mortgage lending is known as a FICO score, ranging from 300-850. According to the three major credit bureau institutions, (Equifax, Experian, and TransUnion), Scores are based upon five broad categories of credit data, including:

- ***Payment history***—35% of your score is based on this category. Lenders look at your overall payment record in making payments to other lenders. Simply, do you pay your bills as agreed? While an occasional late payment is factored into this score, a history of paying on time on most of your credit accounts will help increase your score.
- ***Amounts owed***—30% of your score is based on this category. Having credit accounts and owing money on them does not mean you are a high-risk borrower with a low score. However, owing a great deal on many accounts can indicate that a person is overextended. Lenders are looking to see how many accounts have balances, how much of your total credit line is being used, and how much you still owe on installment loans, such as car loans. Paying

down installment loans and other balances is a good sign that you are able and willing to manage and repay debt.
- ***Length of Credit History***—15% of your score is based on this category. In general, a longer credit history will increase your score; however, a relatively new credit history or only one or two traditional accounts can receive high scores as well.
- ***New Credit***—10% of your score is based on this category. Research shows that opening several credit accounts in a short period of time does represent greater risk—especially for people who do not have a long-established credit history. Your credit score does distinguish between a search for many new credit accounts and rate shopping for one new account. Your score takes into account how many accounts you have, how long it has been since you opened a new account, recent requests for credit, and a good recent credit rating.
- ***Types of Credit***—10% of your score is based on this category. The score will consider your mix of credit cards, retail accounts, installment loans, finance company accounts and mortgage loans. It is not necessary to have one of each and it is never a good idea to open credit accounts you don't intend to use.

Another question is, How do I know what's in my credit report and what my score is?

"It's important to make it your priority to know what's in your credit report. Consumers are entitled to receive one FREE copy of their credit report per bureau per year. You can request a copy of your report online at www.annualcreditreport.com, by calling (877) 322-8228, or by mailing a request form to Annual Credit Report Request Service, P.O. Box 105281, Atlanta, GA 30348-5281. It is a good idea to request a copy from each of the three bureaus—Equifax, Experian and Trans-Union. Each compiles data slightly differently and one could include erroneous information not on the others. In order to access your report, you will need to provide your name, social security number, date of birth, and information only you would know, such as the amount of a monthly mortgage or car payment. When requesting your free credit report, you will also have the option to purchase a report that contains your credit score. You can also purchase your FICO score directly from Fair Isaac at www.myfico.com.

Your next question may be, How do I deal with incorrect information on my report?

Once you've received a copy of your credit report, you may find that certain things aren't accurate. As you review your credit report, if you find inaccurate information or feel that the report gives a misleading picture of past credit problems that have since been resolved, you can write to the reporting agencies asking them to correct your record. Be sure to provide any documentation that supports your claim. If you have an unresolved dispute with a creditor, the credit agency must include your explanation of the situation in future credit reports.

The question I've been asked the most is, How can I improve my credit score?

There are lots of ways to maintain a good credit score and to improve one that is the result of past financial struggles. **Fair Isaac** offers the following tips for raising your score:

- Pay your bills on time
- If you have missed payments, get current and stay current
- Be aware that paying off a collection account, or closing an account on which you previously missed a payment, will not remove it from your credit report.
- If you are having trouble making ends meet, contact your creditors or see a legitimate credit counselor. Seeing a counselor can put you on the path to raising your score, and you won't lose points for seeking help.
- Keep balances low on credit cards and other "revolving credit."
- Pay off debt rather than moving it around.
- Don't close unused credit cards as a short-term strategy to raise your score.
- Don't open a number of new credit cards that you don't need, just to increase your available credit.
- If you have been managing credit for a short time, don't open a lot of new accounts too rapidly.
- Do your shopping for a given automobile or mortgage loan within a focused period of time. Personally, I prefer 15 days.

- Re-establish your credit history if you have had problems.
- Note that it's OK to request your own credit report and your own FICO score without affecting your score.
- Apply for and open new credit accounts only as needed.
- Have credit cards—but manage them responsibly.
- Note that closing an account doesn't make it go away.

The important thing to remember is that it doesn't take much for your score to be affected. Be very careful of your inquiries, your purchases, and your payment habits. As scary as it sounds ... someone is always watching.

Requesting your credit report

The information in your credit report determines in large part what kind of credit, you'll be able to get. This could range anywhere from credit cards to car loans to mortgages. Federal law gives you the right to know what consumer credit information is collected on you and you need to exercise that right.

You should check your credit report periodically to ensure that all the information is correct and to guard yourself against your credit being stolen by identity thieves. You can be very aggressive with your credit management and pull your score with some regularity. Or you can take a more passive approach, checking once a year to see the status of your credit. This may boil down

Small Sacrifice, Huge Harvest

to your personality type. Regardless of which approach you take, it's not hard to get a copy of your credit report.

There are three major credit reporting bureaus: Experian, TransUnion and Equifax. You should get a copy of your report from each. Depending on where you live and your credit history, you should be able to get at least one free copy a year.

You can request a copy online; the links below will allow you to access each company's Web site where you can get more details on obtaining your credit report. Make a separate request of each agency.

Many people, however, prefer the old-fashioned mail system when it comes to dealing with transmission of personal financial data. If you are more comfortable asking for a copy via a letter, then simply use this form and send a separate letter to each agency.

Personalize the letter by entering your specifics in red so it stands out as urgent. I've provided a sample in this book for you.

Equifax Credit Information Services Inc
P.O. Box 740241 Atlanta, GA 30374
www.equifax.com

TransUnion LLC
Consumer Disclosure Center P.O. Box 1000 Chester, PA 19022
www.transunion.com

Experian
National Consumer Assistance Center P.O. Box 2002 Allen, TX 75013
www.experian.com

Natalie Smith, MBA

Sample Credit Report Request Letter

Address of Credit bureau

Re: Requesting a credit report

Dear Sir or Madam:

In accordance with the Federal Fair Credit Reporting Act, I am sending this letter to request a copy of my credit report.

To expedite my request, here is my personal information:
- Your full name
- Your Social Security number
- Your date of birth
- Your full address (street, city, state, ZIP Code)
- Your home telephone number

Please include all sources for the information and the complete records of any distribution of credit information to any parties by any sources.

Enclosed, you will find my payment of [insert amount] to cover cost of the report.

(If you are seeking a copy of your credit report because you recently were denied credit, mention that here. You are entitled to a free copy of your credit report if you request it within 60 days of the date that a creditor said "no" because of something in your file. Let the credit agency know that's why you want your report, see below, if this is applicable)

On [insert specific date] I was declined credit by [Insert name of creditor]. Enclosed you will find a copy

Small Sacrifice, Huge Harvest

of the letter from the creditor refusing me credit. Please do not share this information with any other agency.

(Any other details you would like to add about the report or your credit in general should be detailed here).

Thank you for your prompt attention to my request.

Your Signature
Your Typed Name Your Address City, State and ZIP Code

Chapter 8

Money Saving Tips

Saving on Home Expense

1. For return on investment, the best home renovation is to upgrade an old bathroom. Kitchens come in second.
2. It's worth refinancing your mortgage when you can cut your interest rate by at least one point.
3. Spend no more than 2 1/2 times your income on a home. For a down payment, it's best to come up with at least 20%.
4. Your total housing payments should not exceed 28% of your gross income. Total debt payments should come in under 36%.
5. Think twice before hiring a home improvement contractor who solicits door to door.

Saving on Investments

6. All else being equal, a wise place to invest is a 401(k). Once you've earned the full company match, max out a Roth IRA. Still have money to invest? Put more in your 401(k) or a traditional IRA.

7. Aim to build a retirement nest egg that is 25 times the annual investment income you need. So if you want $40,000 a year to supplement Social Security and a pension, you must save $1 million.
8. If you don't understand how an investment works, don't buy it.

Saving by Planning

9. If you're not saving 10% of your salary, you aren't saving enough.
10. Keep three months' worth of living expenses in a bank savings account or a money-market fund for emergencies. If you have kids or rely on one income, make it six months'.
11. Aim to accumulate enough money to pay for a third of your kids' college costs. You can borrow the rest or cover it from your income.
12. You need enough life insurance to replace at least five years of your salary—as much as 10 years if you have several young children or significant debts.
13. When you buy insurance, choose the highest deductible you can afford. It's the easiest way to lower your premium.
14. The best credit card is a no-fee rewards card that you pay in full every month. But if you carry a balance, high interest rates will wipe out the benefits.
15. The best way to improve your credit score is to pay bills on time and to borrow no more than 30% of your available credit.

Small Sacrifice, Huge Harvest

16. Anyone who calls or e-mails you asking for your Social Security number or information about your bank or credit-card account is a scam artist.

Saving while Spending

17. The best way to save money on a car is to buy a late-model used car and drive it until it's junk. A car loses 30% of its value in the first year.
18. Lease a new car or truck only if you plan to replace it within two or three years.
19. Resist the urge to buy the latest computer or other gadget as soon as it comes out. Wait a few months and the price will be lower.
20. Buy airline tickets early because the cheapest fares are snapped up first. Most seats go on sale several months in advance.
21. When you shop for electronics, don't pay for an extended warranty. One exception: It's a laptop and the warranty is from the manufacturer.

Chapter 9

One of My Favorite Pass-Times

If I'm not careful, I could spend the entire day just reading various quotes. I find them so enlightening. Sometimes when I'm exhausted and I don't feel like reading a self help book, I just look up quotes. I find that I gain so much insight from just a simple line. Along with the insight, there's usually a chuckle or two that may follow, because they're often funny one-liners. I've decided to share some of my favorites with you. As People have been arguing and agonizing over money for thousands of years. Here are some of the choice quotes to lighten the mood. I do hope you enjoy them.

Famous Financial Quotes

1. "Money will come when you are doing the right thing." - Mike Phillips
2. The bank hath benefit of interest on all moneys which it creates out of nothing. ~William Paterson (founder of Bank of England 1694)
3. Today, there are three kinds of people: the haves, the have-nots, and the have-not-paid-for-what-they-haves. ~Earl Wilson

4. A tragic irony of life is that we so often achieve success or financial independence after the chief reason for which we sought it has passed away. ~Ellen Glasgow
5. As a novelist, I tell stories and people give me money. Then financial planners tell me stories and I give them money. ~Martin Cruz Smith
6. Derivatives are financial weapons of mass destruction. ~Warren Buffett
7. The safe way to double your money is to fold it over once and put it in your pocket. ~Frank Hubbard
8. Only when the last tree has died and the last river been poisoned and the last fish been caught will we realize we cannot eat money. ~Cree Indian Proverb
9. The only reason a great many American families don't own an elephant is that they have never been offered an elephant for a dollar down and easy weekly payments. ~Mad Magazine
10. A bank is a place that will lend you money if you can prove that you don't need it. ~Bob Hope
11. Business is the art of extracting money from another man's pocket without resorting to violence. ~Max Amsterdam
12. If you lend someone $20, and never see that person again, it was probably worth it. ~Author Unknown
13. The only thing that can console one for being poor is extravagance. ~Oscar Wilde
14. Money isn't the most important thing in life, but it's reasonably close to oxygen on the "gotta have it" scale. ~Zig Ziglar

Small Sacrifice, Huge Harvest

15. People are living longer than ever before, a phenomenon undoubtedly made necessary by the 30-year mortgage. ~Doug Larson
16. A man is usually more careful of his money than of his principles. ~Oliver Wendell Holmes, Jr., speech, Boston, 8 January 1897

One man that was infamous for his quotes was Benjamin Franklin. Here are a few that keep my wheels spinning:

17. To the generous mind, the heaviest debt is that of gratitude when it is not in our power to repay it.
18. Rather go to bed without dinner than to rise in debt. Many a man thinks he is buying pleasure, when he is really selling himself to it.
19. It is only when the rich are sick that they fully feel the importance of wealth.
20. It is the eye of other people that ruin us. If I were blind I would want, neither fine clothes, fine houses, or fine furniture.
21. Money has never made man happy, nor will it, there is nothing in its nature to produce happiness. The more of it one has the more one wants.
22. If you would know the value of money, go and try to borrow some. He that waits upon fortune, is never sure of a dinner.
23. Gain may be temporary and uncertain; but ever while you live, expense is constant and certain: and it is easier to build two chimneys than to keep one in fuel.
24. Creditors have better memories than debtors.

25. Content makes poor men rich; discontent makes rich men poor.
26. An investment in knowledge pays the best interest.
27. A penny saved is a penny earned.
28. If you know how to spend less than you get, you have the philosopher's stone.

Quotes that have literally forced me to overcome obstacles and keep moving forward:

28. Find a way or make a way. Clark Atlanta University
29. Either roll with me . . . or get rolled over. Random Lecturer

Glossary specific to Credit and Mortgage Terms

A

"A" Loan or "A" Paper: a credit rating where the FICO score is 660 or above. There have been no late mortgage payments within a 12-month period. This is the best credit rating to have when entering into a new loan.

ARM: Adjustable Rate Mortgage; a mortgage loan subject to changes in interest rates; when rates change, ARM monthly payments increase or decrease at intervals determined by the lender; the change in monthly payment amount, however, is usually subject to a cap.

Abstract of Title: documents recording the ownership of property throughout time.

Acceleration: the right of the lender to demand payment on the outstanding balance of a loan.

Acceptance: the written approval of the buyer's offer by the seller.

Additional Principal Payment: money paid to the lender in addition to the established payment amount used directly against the loan principal to shorten the length of the loan.

Adjustable-Rate Mortgage (ARM): a mortgage loan that does not have a fixed interest rate. During the life of the loan the interest rate will change based on the index rate. Also referred to as adjustable mortgage loans (AMLs) or variable-rate mortgages (VRMs).

Adjustment Date: the actual date that the interest rate is changed for an ARM.

Adjustment Index: the published market index used to calculate the interest rate of an ARM at the time of origination or adjustment.

Adjustment Interval: the time between the interest rate change and the monthly payment for an ARM. The interval is usually every one, three or five years depending on the index.

Affidavit: a signed, sworn statement made by the buyer or seller regarding the truth of information provided.

Amenity: a feature of the home or property that serves as a benefit to the buyer but that is not necessary to its use; may be natural (like location, woods, water) or man-made (like a swimming pool or garden).

American Society of Home Inspectors: the American Society of Home Inspectors is a professional association of independent home inspectors. Phone: (800) 743-2744

Amortization: a payment plan that enables you to reduce your debt gradually through monthly payments. The payments may be principal and interest, or interest-only. The monthly amount is based on the schedule for the entire term or length of the loan.

Annual Mortgagor Statement: yearly statement to borrowers detailing the remaining principal and amounts paid for taxes and interest.

Annual Percentage Rate (APR): a measure of the cost of credit, expressed as a yearly rate. It includes interest as well as other charges. Because all lenders, by federal law, follow the same rules to ensure the accuracy of the annual percentage rate, it provides consumers with a good basis for comparing the cost of loans, including mortgage plans. APR is a higher rate than the simple interest of the mortgage.

Application: the first step in the official loan approval process; this form is used to record important information about the potential borrower necessary to the underwriting process.

Application Fee: a fee charged by lenders to process a loan application.

Appraisal: a document from a professional that gives an estimate of a property's fair market value based on the sales of comparable homes in the area and the features of a property; an appraisal is generally required by a lender before loan approval to ensure that the mortgage loan amount is not more than the value of the property.

Appraisal Fee: fee charged by an appraiser to estimate the market value of a property.

Appraised Value: an estimation of the current market value of a property.

Appraiser: a qualified individual who uses his or her experience and knowledge to prepare the appraisal estimate.

Appreciation: an increase in property value.

Arbitration: a legal method of resolving a dispute without going to court.

As-is Condition: the purchase or sale of a property in its existing condition without repairs.

Asking Price: a seller's stated price for a property.

Assessed Value: the value that a public official has placed on any asset (used to determine taxes).

Assessments: the method of placing value on an asset for taxation purposes.

Assessor: a government official who is responsible for determining the value of a property for the purpose of taxation.

Assets: any item with measurable value.

Assumable Mortgage: when a home is sold, the seller may be able to transfer the mortgage to the new buyer. This means the mortgage is assumable. Lenders generally require a credit review of the new borrower and may charge a fee for the assumption. Some mortgages contain a due-on-sale clause, which means that the mortgage may not be transferable to a new buyer. Instead, the lender may make you pay the entire balance that is due when you sell the home. An assumable mortgage can help you attract buyers if you sell your home.

Assumption Clause: a provision in the terms of a loan that allows the buyer to take legal responsibility for the mortgage from the seller.

Automated Underwriting: loan processing completed through a computer-based system that evaluates past credit history to determine if a loan should be approved. This system removes the possibility of personal bias against the buyer.

Average Price: determining the cost of a home by totaling the cost of all houses sold in one area and dividing by the number of homes sold.

B

"B" Loan or "B" Paper: FICO scores from 620 - 659. Factors include two 30 day late mortgage payments and two to three 30 day late installment loan payments in the last 12 months. No delinquencies over 60 days are allowed. Should be two to four years since a bankruptcy. Also referred to as Sub-Prime.

Back End Ratio (debt ratio): a ratio that compares the total of all monthly debt payments (mortgage, real estate taxes and insurance, car loans, and other consumer loans) to gross monthly income.

Back to Back Escrow: arrangements that an owner makes to oversee the sale of one property and the purchase of another at the same time.

Balance Sheet: a financial statement that shows the assets, liabilities and net worth of an individual or company.

Balloon Loan or Mortgage: a mortgage that typically offers low rates for an initial period of time (usually 5, 7, or 10) years; after that time period elapses, the balance is due or is refinanced by the borrower.

Balloon Payment: the final lump sum payment due at the end of a balloon mortgage.

Bankruptcy: a federal law whereby a person's assets are turned over to a trustee and used to pay off outstanding debts; this usually occurs when someone owes more than they have the ability to repay.

Biweekly Payment Mortgage: a mortgage paid twice a month instead of once a month, reducing the amount of interest to be paid on the loan.

Borrower: a person who has been approved to receive a loan and is then obligated to repay it and any additional fees according to the loan terms.

Bridge Loan: a short-term loan paid back relatively fast. Normally used until a long-term loan can be processed.

Broker: a licensed individual or firm that charges a fee to serve as the mediator between the buyer and seller. Mortgage brokers are individuals in the business of arranging funding or negotiating contracts for a client, but who does not loan the money. A real estate broker is someone who helps find a house.

Building Code: based on agreed upon safety standards within a specific area, a building code is a regulation that determines the design, construction, and materials used in building.

Budget: a detailed record of all income earned and spent during a specific period of time.

Buy Down: the seller pays an amount to the lender so the lender provides a lower rate and lower payments many times for an ARM. The seller may increase the sales price to cover the cost of the buy down.

C

"C" Loan or "C" Paper: FICO scores typically from 580 to 619. Factors include three to four 30 day late mortgage payments and four to six 30 day late installment loan payments or two to four 60 day late payments. Should be one to two years since bankruptcy. Also referred to as Sub - Prime.

Small Sacrifice, Huge Harvest

Callable Debt: a debt security whose issuer has the right to redeem the security at a specified price on or after a specified date, but prior to its stated final maturity.

Cap: a limit, such as one placed on an adjustable rate mortgage, on how much a monthly payment or interest rate can increase or decrease, either at each adjustment period or during the life of the mortgage. Payment caps do not limit the amount of interest the lender is earning, so they may cause negative amortization.

Capacity: The ability to make mortgage payments on time, dependant on assets and the amount of income each month after paying housing costs, debts and other obligations.

Capital Gain: the profit received based on the difference of the original purchase price and the total sale price.

Capital Improvements: property improvements that either will enhance the property value or will increase the useful life of the property.

Capital or Cash Reserves: an individual's savings, investments, or assets.

Cash-Out Refinance: when a borrower refinances a mortgage at a higher principal amount to get additional money. Usually this occurs when the property has appreciated in value. For example, if a home has a current value of $100,000 and an outstanding mortgage of $60,000, the owner could refinance $80,000 and have additional $20,000 in cash.

Cash Reserves: a cash amount sometimes required of the buyer to be held in reserve in addition to the down payment and closing costs; the amount is determined by the lender.

Casualty Protection: property insurance that covers any damage to the home and personal property either inside or outside the home.

Certificate of Title: a document provided by a qualified source, such as a title company, that shows the property legally belongs to the current owner; before the title is transferred at closing, it should be clear and free of all liens or other claims.

Chapter 7 Bankruptcy: a bankruptcy that requires assets be liquidated in exchange for the cancellation of debt.

Chapter 13 Bankruptcy: this type of bankruptcy sets a payment plan between the borrower and the creditor monitored by the court. The homeowner can keep the property, but must make payments according to the court's terms within a 3 to 5 year period.

Charge-Off: the portion of principal and interest due on a loan that is written off when deemed to be uncollectible.

Clear Title: a property title that has no defects. Properties with clear titles are marketable for sale.

Closing: the final step in property purchase where the title is transferred from the seller to the buyer. Closing occurs at a meeting between the buyer, seller, settlement agent, and other agents. At the closing the seller receives payment for the property. Also known as settlement.

Closing Costs: fees for final property transfer not included in the price of the property. Typical closing costs include charges for the mortgage loan such as origination fees, discount points, appraisal fee, survey, title insurance, legal fees, real estate professional fees, prepayment of taxes and insurance, and real estate transfer taxes. A common estimate of a Buyer's closing costs is 2 to 4 percent of the purchase price of the home. A common estimate for Seller's closing costs is 3 to 9 percent.

Cloud On The Title: any condition which affects the clear title to real property.

Co-Borrower: an additional person that is responsible for loan repayment and is listed on the title.

Co-Signed Account: an account signed by someone in addition to the primary borrower, making both people responsible for the amount borrowed.

Co-Signer: a person that signs a credit application with another person, agreeing to be equally responsible for the repayment of the loan.

Collateral: security in the form of money or property pledged for the payment of a loan. For example, on a home loan, the home is the collateral and can be taken away from the borrower if mortgage payments are not made.

Collection Account: an unpaid debt referred to a collection agency to collect on the bad debt. This type of account is reported to the credit bureau and will show on the borrower's credit report.

Commission: an amount, usually a percentage of the property sales price that is collected by a real estate professional as a fee for negotiating the transaction. Traditionally the home seller pays the commission. The amount of commission is determined by the real estate professional and the seller and can be as much as 6% of the sales price.

Common Stock: a security that provides voting rights in a corporation and pays a dividend after preferred stock holders have been paid. This is the most common stock held within a company.

Comparative Market Analysis (COMPS): a property evaluation that determines property value by comparing similar properties sold within the last year.

Compensating Factors: factors that show the ability to repay a loan based on less traditional criteria, such as employment, rent, and utility payment history.

Condominium: a form of ownership in which individuals purchase and own a unit of housing in a multi-unit complex. The owner also shares financial responsibility for common areas.

Conforming loan: is a loan that does not exceed Fannie Mae's and Freddie Mac's loan limits. Freddie Mac and Fannie Mae loans are referred to as conforming loans.

Consideration: an item of value given in exchange for a promise or act.

Construction Loan: a short-term, to finance the cost of building a new home. The lender pays the builder based on milestones accomplished during the building process. For example, once a sub-contractor pours the foundation and it is approved by inspectors the lender will pay for their service.

Contingency: a clause in a purchase contract outlining conditions that must be fulfilled before the contract is executed. Both, buyer or seller may include contingencies in a contract, but both parties must accept the contingency.

Conventional Loan: a private sector loan, one that is not guaranteed or insured by the U.S. government.

Small Sacrifice, Huge Harvest

Conversion Clause: a provision in some ARMs allowing it to change to a fixed-rate loan at some point during the term. Usually conversions are allowed at the end of the first adjustment period. At the time of the conversion, the new fixed rate is generally set at one of the rates then prevailing for fixed rate mortgages. There may be additional cost for this clause.

Convertible ARM: an adjustable-rate mortgage that provides the borrower the ability to convert to a fixed-rate within a specified time.

Cooperative (Co-op): residents purchase stock in a cooperative corporation that owns a structure; each stockholder is then entitled to live in a specific unit of the structure and is responsible for paying a portion of the loan.

Cost of Funds Index (COFI): an index used to determine interest rate changes for some adjustable-rate mortgages.

Counter Offer: a rejection to all or part of a purchase offer that negotiates different terms to reach an acceptable sales contract.

Covenants: legally enforceable terms that govern the use of property. These terms are transferred with the property deed. Discriminatory covenants are illegal and unenforceable. Also known as a condition, restriction, deed restriction or restrictive covenant.

Credit: an agreement that a person will borrow money and repay it to the lender over time.

Credit Bureau: an agency that provides financial information and payment history to lenders about potential borrowers. Also known as a National Credit Repository.

Credit Counseling: education on how to improve bad credit and how to avoid having more debt than can be repaid.

Credit Enhancement: a method used by a lender to reduce default of a loan by requiring collateral, mortgage insurance, or other agreements.

Credit Grantor: the lender that provides a loan or credit.

Credit History: a record of an individual that lists all debts and the payment history for each. The report that is generated from the history is called a credit report. Lenders use this information to gauge a potential borrower's ability to repay a loan.

Credit Loss Ratio: the ratio of credit-related losses to the dollar amount of MBS outstanding and total mortgages owned by the corporation.

Credit Related Expenses: foreclosed property expenses plus the provision for losses.

Credit Related Losses: foreclosed property expenses combined with charge-offs.

Credit Repair Companies: Private, for-profit businesses that claim to offer consumers credit and debt repayment difficulties assistance with their credit problems and a bad credit report.

Credit Report: a report generated by the credit bureau that contains the borrower's credit history for the past seven years. Lenders use this information to determine if a loan will be granted.

Credit Risk: a term used to describe the possibility of default on a loan by a borrower.

Credit Score: a score calculated by using a person's credit report to determine the likelihood of a loan being repaid on time. Scores range from about 360 - 840: a lower score meaning a person is a higher risk, while a higher score means that there is less risk.

Credit Union: a non-profit financial institution federally regulated and owned by the members or people who use their services. Credit unions serve groups that hold a common interest and you have to become a member to use the available services.

Creditor: the lending institution providing a loan or credit.

Creditworthiness: the way a lender measures the ability of a person to qualify and repay a loan.

D

Debtor: The person or entity that borrows money. The term debtor may be used interchangeably with the term borrower.

Debt-to-Income Ratio: a comparison or ratio of gross income to housing and non-housing expenses; With the FHA, the-monthly mortgage payment should be no more than 29% of monthly gross income (before taxes) and the mortgage payment combined with non-housing debts should not exceed 41% of income.

Debt Security: a security that represents a loan from an investor to an issuer. The issuer in turn agrees to pay interest in addition to the principal amount borrowed.

Deductible: the amount of cash payment that is made by the insured (the homeowner) to cover a portion of a damage or loss. Sometimes also called "out-of-pocket expenses." For example, out of a total damage claim of $1,000, the homeowner might pay a $250 deductible toward the loss, while the insurance company pays $750 toward the loss. Typically, the higher the deductible, the lower the cost of the policy.

Deed: a document that legally transfers ownership of property from one person to another. The deed is recorded on public record with the property description and the owner's signature. Also known as the title.

Deed-in-Lieu: to avoid foreclosure ("in lieu" of foreclosure), a deed is given to the lender to fulfill the obligation to repay the debt; this process does not allow the borrower to remain in the house but helps avoid the costs, time, and effort associated with foreclosure.

Default: the inability to make timely monthly mortgage payments or otherwise comply with mortgage terms. A loan is considered in default when payment has not been paid after 60 to 90 days. Once in default the lender can exercise legal rights defined in the contract to begin foreclosure proceedings

Delinquency: failure of a borrower to make timely mortgage payments under a loan agreement. Generally after fifteen days a late fee may be assessed.

Deposit (Earnest Money): money put down by a potential buyer to show that they are serious about purchasing the home; it becomes part of the down payment if the offer is accepted, is returned if the offer is rejected, or is forfeited if the buyer pulls out of the deal. During the contingency period the money may be returned to the buyer if the contingencies are not met to the buyer's satisfaction.

Depreciation: a decrease in the value or price of a property due to changes in market conditions, wear and tear on the property, or other factors.

Derivative: a contract between two or more parties where the security is dependent on the price of another investment.

Disclosures: the release of relevant information about a property that may influence the final sale, especially if it represents defects or problems. "Full disclosure" usually refers to the responsibility of the seller to voluntarily provide all known information about the property. Some disclosures may be required by law, such as the federal requirement to warn of potential lead-based paint hazards in pre-1978 housing. A seller found to have knowingly lied about a defect may face legal penalties.

Discount Point: normally paid at closing and generally calculated to be equivalent to 1% of the total loan amount, discount points are paid to reduce the interest rate on a loan. In an ARM with an initial rate discount, the lender gives up a number of percentage points in interest to give you a lower rate and lower payments for part of the mortgage term (usually for one year or less). After the discount period, the ARM rate will probably go up depending on the index rate.

Down Payment: the portion of a home's purchase price that is paid in cash and is not part of the mortgage loan. This amount varies based on the loan type, but is determined by taking the difference of the sale price and the actual mortgage loan amount. Mortgage insurance is required when a down payment less than 20 percent is made.

Document Recording: after closing on a loan, certain documents are filed and made public record. Discharges for the prior mortgage holder are filed first. Then the deed is filed with the new owner's and mortgage company's names.

Due on Sale Clause: a provision of a loan allowing the lender to demand full repayment of the loan if the property is sold.

Duration: the number of years it will take to receive the present value of all future payments on a security to include both principal and interest.

E

Earnest Money (Deposit): money put down by a potential buyer to show that they are serious about purchasing the home; it becomes part of the down payment if the offer is accepted, is returned if the offer is rejected, or is forfeited if the buyer pulls out of the deal. During the contingency period the money may be returned to the buyer if the contingencies are not met to the buyer's satisfaction.

Earnings Per Share (EPS): a corporation's profit that is divided among each share of common stock. It is determined by taking the net earnings divided by the number of outstanding common stocks held. This is a way that a company reports profitability.

Easements: the legal rights that give someone other than the owner access to use property for a specific purpose. Easements may affect property values and are sometimes a part of the deed.

EEM: Energy Efficient Mortgage; an FHA program that helps homebuyers save money on utility bills by enabling them to finance the cost of adding energy efficiency features to a new or existing home as part of the home purchase

Eminent Domain: when a government takes private property for public use. The owner receives payment for its fair market value. The property can then proceed to condemnation proceedings.

Encroachments: a structure that extends over the legal property line on to another individual's property. The property surveyor will note any encroachment on the lot survey done before property transfer. The person who owns the structure will be asked to remove it to prevent future problems.

Encumbrance: anything that affects title to a property, such as loans, leases, easements, or restrictions.

Equal Credit Opportunity Act (ECOA): a federal law requiring lenders to make credit available equally without discrimination based on race, color, religion, national origin, age, sex, marital status, or receipt of income from public assistance programs.

Equity: an owner's financial interest in a property; calculated by subtracting the amount still owed on the mortgage loan(s) from the fair market value of the property.

Escape Clause: a provision in a purchase contract that allows either party to cancel part or the entire contract if the other does not respond to changes to the sale within a set period. The most common use of the escape clause is if the buyer makes the purchase offer contingent on the sale of another house.

Escrow: funds held in an account to be used by the lender to pay for home insurance and property taxes.

The funds may also be held by a third party until contractual conditions are met and then paid out.

Escrow Account: a separate account into which the lender puts a portion of each monthly mortgage payment; an escrow account provides the funds needed for such expenses as property taxes, homeowners insurance, mortgage insurance, etc.

Estate: the ownership interest of a person in real property. The sum total of all property, real and personal, owned by a person.

Exclusive Listing: a written contract giving a real estate agent the exclusive right to sell a property for a specific timeframe.

F

FICO Score: FICO is an abbreviation for Fair Isaac Corporation and refers to a person's credit score based on credit history. Lenders and credit card companies use the number to decide if the person is likely to pay his or her bills. A credit score is evaluated using information from the three major credit bureaus and is usually between 300 and 850.

FSBO (For Sale by Owner): a home that is offered for sale by the owner without the benefit of a real estate professional.

Fair Credit Reporting Act: federal act to ensure that credit bureaus are fair and accurate protecting the individual's privacy rights enacted in 1971 and revised in October 1997.

Fair Housing Act: a law that prohibits discrimination in all facets of the home buying process on the basis of race, color, national origin, religion, sex, familial status, or disability.

Fair Market Value: the hypothetical price that a willing buyer and seller will agree upon when they are acting freely, carefully, and with complete knowledge of the situation.

Familial Status: HUD uses this term to describe a single person, a pregnant woman or a household with children under 18 living with parents or legal custodians who might experience housing discrimination.

Fannie Mae: Federal National Mortgage Association (FNMA); a federally-chartered enterprise owned by private stockholders that purchases residential mortgages and converts them into securities for sale to investors; by purchasing mortgages, Fannie Mae supplies funds that lenders may loan to potential homebuyers. Also known as a Government Sponsored Enterprise (GSE).

FHA: Federal Housing Administration; established in 1934 to advance homeownership opportunities for all Americans; assists homebuyers by providing mortgage insurance to lenders to cover most losses that may occur when a borrower defaults; this encourages lenders to make loans to borrowers who might not qualify for conventional mortgages.

First Mortgage: the mortgage with first priority if the loan is not paid.

Fixed Expenses: payments that do not vary from month to month.

Fixed-Rate Mortgage: a mortgage with payments that remain the same throughout the life of the loan because the interest rate and other terms are fixed and do not change.

Fixture: personal property permanently attached to real estate or real property that becomes a part of the real estate.

Float: the act of allowing an interest rate and discount points to fluctuate with changes in the market.

Flood Insurance: insurance that protects homeowners against losses from a flood; if a home is located in a flood plain, the lender will require flood insurance before approving a loan.

Forbearance: a lender may decide not to take legal action when a borrower is late in making a payment. Usually this occurs when a borrower sets up a plan that both sides agree will bring overdue mortgage payments up to date.

Foreclosure: a legal process in which mortgaged property is sold to pay the loan of the defaulting borrower. Foreclosure laws are based on the statutes of each state.

Freddie Mac: Federal Home Loan Mortgage Corporation (FHLM); a federally chartered corporation that purchases residential mortgages, securitizes them, and sells them to investors; this provides lenders with funds for new homebuyers. Also known as a Government Sponsored Enterprise (GSE).

Front End Ratio: a percentage comparing a borrower's total monthly cost to buy a house (mortgage principal and interest, insurance, and real estate taxes) to monthly income before deductions.

G

GSE: abbreviation for government sponsored enterprises: a collection of financial services corporations formed by the United States Congress to reduce interest rates for farmers and homeowners. Examples include Fannie Mae and Freddie Mac.

Ginnie Mae: Government National Mortgage Association (GNMA); a government-owned corporation overseen by the U.S. Department of Housing and Urban Development, Ginnie Mae pools FHA-insured and VA-guaranteed loans to back securities for private investment; as With Fannie Mae and Freddie Mac, the investment income provides funding that may then be lent to eligible borrowers by lenders.

Global Debt Facility: designed to allow investors all over the world to purchase debt (loans) of U.S. dollar and foreign currency through a variety of clearing systems.

Good Faith Estimate: an estimate of all closing fees including pre-paid and escrow items as well as lender charges; must be given to the borrower within three days after submission of a loan application.

Graduated Payment Mortgages: mortgages that begin with lower monthly payments that get slowly larger over a period of years, eventually reaching a fixed level and remaining there for the life of the loan. Graduated payment loans may be good if you expect your annual income to increase.

Grantee: an individual to whom an interest in real property is conveyed.

Grantor: an individual conveying an interest in real property.

Gross Income: money earned before taxes and other deductions. Sometimes it may include income from self-employment, rental property, alimony, child support, public assistance payments, and retirement benefits.

Guaranty Fee: payment to FannieMae from a lender for the assurance of timely principal and interest payments to MBS (Mortgage Backed Security) security holders.

H

HECM (Reverse Mortgage): the reverse mortgage is used by senior homeowners age 62 and older to convert the equity in their home into monthly streams of income and/or a line of credit to be repaid when they no longer occupy the home. A lending institution such as a mortgage lender, bank, credit union or savings and loan association funds the FHA insured loan, commonly known as HECM.

Hazard Insurance: protection against a specific loss, such as fire, wind etc., over a period of time that is secured by the payment of a regularly scheduled premium.

HELP: Homebuyer Education Learning Program; an educational program from the FHA that counsels people about the home buying process; HELP covers topics like budgeting, finding a home, getting a loan, and home maintenance; in most cases, completion of the program may entitle the homebuyer to a reduced initial FHA mortgage insurance premium-from 2.25% to 1.75% of the home purchase price.

Home Equity Line of Credit: a mortgage loan, usually in second mortgage, allowing a borrower to obtain cash against the equity of a home, up to a predetermined amount.

Home Equity Loan: a loan backed by the value of a home (real estate). If the borrower defaults or does not pay the loan, the lender has some rights to the property. The borrower can usually claim a home equity loan as a tax deduction. Home Inspection: an examination of the structure and mechanical systems to determine a home's quality, soundness and safety; makes the potential homebuyer aware of any repairs that may be needed. The homebuyer generally pays inspection fees.

Home Warranty: offers protection for mechanical systems and attached appliances against unexpected repairs not covered by homeowner's insurance; coverage extends over a specific time period and does not cover the home's structure.

Homeowner's Insurance: an insurance policy, also called hazard insurance, that combines protection against damage to a dwelling and its contents including fire, storms or other damages with protection against claims of negligence or inappropriate action that result in someone's injury or property damage. Most lenders require homeowners insurance and may escrow the cost. Flood insurance is generally not included in standard policies and must be purchased separately.

Homeownership Education Classes: classes that stress the need to develop a strong credit history and offer information about how to get a mortgage approved, qualify for a loan, choose an affordable home, go through financing and closing processes, and avoid mortgage problems that cause people to lose their homes.

Homestead Credit: property tax credit program, offered by some state governments, that provides reductions in property taxes to eligible households.

Housing Counseling Agency: provides counseling and assistance to individuals on a variety of issues, including loan default, fair housing, and home buying.

HUD: the U.S. Department of Housing and Urban Development; established in 1965, HUD works to create a decent home and suitable living environment for all Americans; it does this by addressing housing needs, improving and developing American communities, and enforcing fair housing laws.

HUD1 Statement: also known as the "settlement sheet," or "closing statement" it itemizes all closing costs; must be given to the borrower at or before closing. Items that appear on the statement include real estate commissions, loan fees, points, and escrow amounts.

HVAC: Heating, Ventilation and Air Conditioning; a home's heating and cooling system.

I

Indemnification: to secure against any loss or damage, compensate or give security for reimbursement for loss or damage incurred. A homeowner should negotiate for inclusion of an indemnification provision in a contract with a general contractor or for a separate indemnity agreement protecting the homeowner from harm, loss or damage caused by actions or omissions of the general (and all sub) contractor.

Index: the measure of interest rate changes that the lender uses to decide how much the interest rate of an

ARM will change over time. No one can be sure when an index rate will go up or down. If a lender bases interest rate adjustments on the average value of an index over time, your interest rate would not be as volatile. You should ask your lender how the index for any ARM you are considering has changed in recent years, and where it is reported.

Inflation: the number of dollars in circulation exceeds the amount of goods and services available for purchase; inflation results in a decrease in the dollar's value.

Inflation Coverage: endorsement to a homeowner's policy that automatically adjusts the amount of insurance to compensate for inflationary rises in the home's value. This type of coverage does not adjust for increases in the home's value due to improvements.

Inquiry: a credit report request. Each time a credit application is completed or more credit is requested counts as an inquiry. A large number of inquiries on a credit report can sometimes make a credit score lower.

Interest: a fee charged for the use of borrowing money.

Interest Rate: the amount of interest charged on a monthly loan payment, expressed as a percentage.

Interest Rate Swap: a transaction between two parties where each agrees to exchange payments tied to different interest rates for a specified period of time, generally based on a notional principal amount.

Intermediate Term Mortgage: a mortgage loan with a contractual maturity from the time of purchase equal to or less than 20 years.

Insurance: protection against a specific loss, such as fire, wind etc., over a period of time that is secured by the payment of a regularly scheduled premium.

J

Joint Tenancy (with Rights of Survivorship): two or more owners share equal ownership and rights to the property. If a joint owner dies, his or her share of the property passes to the other owners, without probate. In joint tenancy, ownership of the property cannot be willed to someone who is not a joint owner.

Judgment: a legal decision; when requiring debt repayment, a judgment may include a property lien that secures the creditor's claim by providing a collateral source.

Jumbo Loan: or non-conforming loan, is a loan that exceeds Fannie Mae's and Freddie Mac's loan limits. Freddie Mac and Fannie Mae loans are referred to as conforming loans.

K

L

Late Payment Charges: the penalty the homeowner must pay when a mortgage payment is made after the due date grace period.

Lease: a written agreement between a property owner and a tenant (resident) that stipulates the payment and conditions under which the tenant may occupy a home or apartment and states a specified period of time.

Lease Purchase (Lease Option): assists low to moderate income homebuyers in purchasing a home by allowing them to lease a home with an option to buy; the rent payment is made up of the monthly rental payment plus an additional amount that is credited to an account for use as a down payment.

Lender: A term referring to an person or company that makes loans for real estate purchases. Sometimes referred to as a loan officer or lender.

Lender Option Commitments: an agreement giving a lender the option to deliver loans or securities by a certain date at agreed upon terms.

Liabilities: a person's financial obligations such as long-term / short-term debt, and other financial obligations to be paid.

Liability Insurance: insurance coverage that protects against claims alleging a property owner's negligence or action resulted in bodily injury or damage to another person. It is normally included in homeowner's insurance policies.

Lien: a legal claim against property that must be satisfied when the property is sold. A claim of money against a property, wherein the value of the property is used as security in repayment of a debt. Examples include a mechanic's lien, which might be for the unpaid cost of building supplies, or a tax lien for unpaid property taxes. A lien is a defect on the title and needs to be settled before transfer of ownership. A lien release is a written report of the settlement of a lien and is recorded in the public record as evidence of payment.

Lien Waiver: A document that releases a consumer (homeowner) from any further obligation for payment of a debt once it has been paid in full. Lien waivers typically are used by homeowners who hire a contractor to provide work and materials to prevent any subcontractors or suppliers of materials from filing a lien against the homeowner for nonpayment.

Life Cap: a limit on the range interest rates can increase or decrease over the life of an adjustable-rate mortgage (ARM).

Line of Credit: an agreement by a financial institution such as a bank to extend credit up to a certain amount for a certain time to a specified borrower.

Liquid Asset: a cash asset or an asset that is easily converted into cash.

Listing Agreement: a contract between a seller and a real estate professional to market and sell a home. A listing agreement obligates the real estate professional (or his or her agent) to seek qualified buyers, report all purchase offers and help negotiate the highest possible price and most favorable terms for the property seller.

Loan: money borrowed that is usually repaid with interest.

Loan Acceleration: an acceleration clause in a loan document is a statement in a mortgage that gives the lender the right to demand payment of the entire outstanding balance if a monthly payment is missed.

Loan Fraud: purposely giving incorrect information on a loan application in order to better qualify for a loan; may result in civil liability or criminal penalties.

Loan Officer: a representative of a lending or mortgage company who is responsible for soliciting homebuyers, qualifying and processing of loans. They may also be called lender, loan representative, account executive or loan rep.

Loan Origination Fee: a charge by the lender to cover the administrative costs of making the mortgage. This charge is paid at the closing and varies with the lender and type of loan. A loan origination fee of 1 to 2 percent of the mortgage amount is common.

Loan Servicer: the company that collects monthly mortgage payments and disperses property taxes and insurance payments. Loan servicers also monitor nonperforming loans, contact delinquent borrowers, and notify insurers and investors of potential problems. Loan servicers may be the lender or a specialized company that just handles loan servicing under contract with the lender or the investor who owns the loan.

Loan to Value (LTV) Ratio: a percentage calculated by dividing the amount borrowed by the price or appraised value of the home to be purchased; the higher the LTV, the less cash a borrower is required to pay as down payment.

Lock-In: since interest rates can change frequently, many lenders offer an interest rate lock-in that guarantees a specific interest rate if the loan is closed within a specific time.

Lock-in Period: the length of time that the lender has guaranteed a specific interest rate to a borrower.

Loss Mitigation: a process to avoid foreclosure; the lender tries to help a borrower who has been unable to make loan payments and is in danger of defaulting on his or her loan

M

Mandatory Delivery Commitment: an agreement that a lender will deliver loans or securities by a certain date at agreed-upon terms.

Margin: the number of percentage points the lender adds to the index rate to calculate the ARM interest rate at each adjustment.

Market Value: the amount a willing buyer would pay a willing seller for a home. An appraised value is an estimate of the current fair market value.

Maturity: the date when the principal balance of a loan becomes due and payable.

Median Price: the price of the house that falls in the middle of the total number of homes for sale in that area.

Medium Term Notes: unsecured general obligations of Fannie Mae with maturities of one day or more and with principal and interest payable in U.S. dollars.

Merged Credit Report: raw data pulled from two or more of the major credit-reporting firms.

Mitigation: term usually used to refer to various changes or improvements made in a home; for instance, to reduce the average level of radon.

Modification: when a lender agrees to modify the terms of a mortgage without refinancing the loan.

Mortgage: a lien on the property that secures the Promise to repay a loan. A security agreement between the lender and the buyer in which the property is collateral for the loan. The mortgage gives the lender the right to collect payment on the loan and to foreclose if the loan obligations are not met.

Mortgage Acceleration Clause: a clause allowing a lender, under certain circumstances, demand the entire balance of a loan is repaid in a lump sum. The acceleration clause is usually triggered if the home is sold, title to the property is changed, the loan is refinanced or the borrower defaults on a scheduled payment.

Mortgage-Backed Security (MBS): a Fannie Mae security that represents an undivided interest in a group of mortgages. Principal and interest payments from the individual mortgage loans are grouped and paid out to the MBS holders.

Mortgage Banker: a company that originates loans and resells them to secondary mortgage lenders like Fannie Mae or Freddie Mac.

Mortgage Broker: a firm that originates and processes loans for a number of lenders.

Mortgage Life and Disability Insurance: term life insurance bought by borrowers to pay off a mortgage in the event of death or make monthly payments in the case of disability. The amount of coverage decreases as the principal balance declines. There are many different terms of coverage determining amounts of payments and when payments begin and end.

Mortgage Insurance: a policy that protects lenders against some or most of the losses that can occur when a borrower defaults on a mortgage loan; mortgage insurance is required primarily for borrowers with a down payment of less than 20% of the home's purchase price. Insurance purchased by the buyer to protect the lender in the event of default. Typically purchased for loans with less than 20 percent down payment. The cost of mortgage insurance is usually added to the monthly payment. Mortgage insurance is maintained on conventional loans until the outstanding amount of the loan is less than 80 percent of the value of the house or for a set period of time (7 years is common). Mortgage insurance also is available through a government agency, such as the Federal Housing Administration (FHA) or through companies (Private Mortgage Insurance or PMI).

Mortgage Insurance Premium (MIP): a monthly payment -usually part of the mortgage payment - paid by a borrower for mortgage insurance.

Mortgage Interest Deduction: the interest cost of a mortgage, which is a tax - deductible expense. The interest reduces the taxable income of taxpayers.

Mortgage Modification: a loss mitigation option that allows a borrower to refinance and/or extend the term of the mortgage loan and thus reduce the monthly payments.

Mortgage Note: a legal document obligating a borrower to repay a loan at a stated interest rate during a specified period; the agreement is secured by a mortgage that is recorded in the public records along with the deed.

Mortgage Qualifying Ratio: Used to calculate the maximum amount of funds that an individual traditionally may be able to afford. A typical mortgage qualifying ratio is 28: 36.

Mortgage Score: a score based on a combination of information about the borrower that is obtained from the loan application, the credit report, and property value information. The score is a comprehensive analysis of the borrower's ability to repay a mortgage loan and manage credit.

Mortgagee: the lender in a mortgage agreement. Mortgagor - The borrower in a mortgage agreement.

Mortgagor: the borrower in a mortgage agreement

Multifamily Housing: a building with more than four residential rental units.

Multiple Listing Service (MLS): within the Metro Columbus area, Realtors submit listings and agree to attempt to sell all properties in the MLS. The MLS is a service of the local Columbus Board of Realtors?. The local MLS has a protocol for updating listings and sharing commissions. The MLS offers the advantage of more timely information, availability, and access to houses and other types of property on the market.

N

National Credit Repositories: currently, there are three companies that maintain national credit - reporting databases. These are Equifax, Experian, and Trans Union, referred to as Credit Bureaus.

Negative Amortization: amortization means that monthly payments are large enough to pay the interest and reduce the principal on your mortgage. Negative amortization occurs when the monthly payments do not cover all of the interest cost. The interest cost that isn't covered is added to the unpaid principal balance. This means that even after making many payments, you could owe more than you did at the beginning of the loan. Negative amortization can occur when an ARM has a payment cap that results in monthly payments not high enough to cover the interest due.

Net Income: Your take-home pay, the amount of money that you receive in your paycheck after taxes and deductions.

No Cash Out Refinance: a refinance of an existing loan only for the amount remaining on the mortgage. The borrower does not get any cash against the equity of the home. Also called a "rate and term refinance."

No Cost Loan: there are many variations of a no cost loan. Generally, it is a loan that does not charge for items such as title insurance, escrow fees, settlement fees, appraisal, recording fees or notary fees. It may also offer no points. This lessens the need for upfront cash during the buying process however no cost loans have a higher interest rate.

Nonperforming Asset: an asset such as a mortgage that is not currently accruing interest or which interest is not being paid.

Note: a legal document obligating a borrower to repay a mortgage loan at a stated interest rate over a specified period of time.

Note Rate: the interest rate stated on a mortgage note.

Notice of Default: a formal written notice to a borrower that there is a default on a loan and that legal action is possible.

Notional Principal Amount: the proposed amount which interest rate swap payments are based but generally not paid or received by either party.

Non-Conforming loan: is a loan that exceeds Fannie Mae's and Freddie Mac's loan limits. Freddie Mac and Fannie Mae loans are referred to as conforming loans.

Notary Public: a person who serves as a public official and certifies the authenticity of required signatures on a document by signing and stamping the document.

O

Offer: indication by a potential buyer of a willingness to purchase a home at a specific price; generally put forth in writing.

Original Principal Balance: the total principal owed on a mortgage prior to any payments being made.

Origination: the process of preparing, submitting, and evaluating a loan application; generally includes a credit check, verification of employment, and a property appraisal.

Origination Fee: the charge for originating a loan; is usually calculated in the form of points and paid at closing. One point equals one percent of the loan amount. On a conventional loan, the loan origination fee is the number of points a borrower pays.

Owner Financing: a home purchase where the seller provides all or part of the financing, acting as a lender.

Ownership: ownership is documented by the deed to a property. The type or form of ownership is important if there is a change in the status of the owners or if the property changes ownership.

Owner's Policy: the insurance policy that protects the buyer from title defects.

P

PITI: Principal, Interest, Taxes, and Insurance: the four elements of a monthly mortgage payment; payments of principal and interest go directly towards repaying the loan while the portion that covers taxes and insurance (homeowner's and mortgage, if applicable) goes into an escrow account to cover the fees when they are due.

PITI Reserves: a cash amount that a borrower must have on hand after making a down payment and paying all closing costs for the purchase of a home. The principal, interest, taxes, and insurance (PITI) reserves must equal the amount that the borrower would have to pay for PITI for a predefined number of months.

PMI: Private Mortgage Insurance; privately-owned companies that offer standard and special affordable mortgage insurance programs for qualified borrowers with down payments of less than 20% of a purchase price.

Partial Claim: a loss mitigation option offered by the FHA that allows a borrower, with help from a lender, to get an interest-free loan from HUD to bring their mortgage payments up to date.

Partial Payment: a payment that is less than the total amount owed on a monthly mortgage payment. Normally, lenders do not accept partial payments. The lender may make exceptions during times of difficulty. Contact your lender prior to the due date if a partial payment is needed.

Payment Cap: a limit on how much an ARM's payment may increase, regardless of how much the interest rate increases.

Small Sacrifice, Huge Harvest

Payment Change Date: the date when a new monthly payment amount takes effect on an adjustable-rate mortgage (ARM) or a graduated-payment mortgage (GPM). Generally, the payment change date occurs in the month immediately after the interest rate adjustment date.

Payment Due Date: Contract language specifying when payments are due on money borrowed. The due date is always indicated and means that the payment must be received on or before the specified date. Grace periods prior to assessing a late fee or additional interest do not eliminate the responsibility of making payments on time.

Perils: for homeowner's insurance, an event that can damage the property. Homeowner's insurance may cover the property for a wide variety of perils caused by accidents, nature, or people.

Personal Property: any property that is not real property or attached to real property. For example furniture is not attached however a new light fixture would be considered attached and part of the real property.

Planned Unit Development (PUD): a development that is planned, and constructed as one entity. Generally, there are common features in the homes or lots governed by covenants attached to the deed. Most planned developments have common land and facilities owned and managed by the owner's or neighborhood association. Homeowners usually are required to participate in the association via a payment of annual dues.

Points: a point is equal to one percent of the principal amount of your mortgage. For example, if you get a mortgage for $95,000, one point means you pay $950 to the lender. Lenders frequently charge points in both fixed-rate and adjustable-rate mortgages in order to increase the yield on the mortgage and to cover loan closing costs. These points usually are collected at closing and may be paid by the borrower or the home seller, or may be split between them.

Power of Attorney: a legal document that authorizes another person to act on your behalf. A power of attorney can grant complete authority or can be limited to certain acts or certain periods of time or both.

Pre-Approval: a lender commits to lend to a potential borrower a fixed loan amount based on a completed loan application, credit reports, debt, savings and has been reviewed by an underwriter. The commitment remains as long as the borrower still meets the qualification requirements at the time of purchase. This does not guaranty a loan until the property has passed inspections underwriting guidelines.

Predatory Lending: abusive lending practices that include a mortgage loan to someone who does not have the ability to repay. It also pertains to repeated refinancing of a loan charging high interest and fees each time.

Predictive Variables: The variables that are part of the formula comprising elements of a credit-scoring model. These variables are used to predict a borrower's future credit performance.

Preferred Stock: stock that takes priority over common stock with regard to dividends and liquidation rights. Preferred stockholders typically have no voting rights.

Pre-foreclosure Sale: a procedure in which the borrower is allowed to sell a property for an amount less than what is owed on it to avoid a foreclosure. This sale fully satisfies the borrower's debt.

Prepayment: any amount paid to reduce the principal balance of a loan before the due date or payment in full of a mortgage. This can occur with the sale of the property, the pay off the loan in full, or a foreclosure. In each case, full payment occurs before the loan has been fully amortized.

Prepayment Penalty: a provision in some loans that charge a fee to a borrower who pays off a loan before it is due.

Pre-Foreclosure sale: allows a defaulting borrower to sell the mortgaged property to satisfy the loan and avoid foreclosure.

Pre-Qualify: a lender informally determines the maximum amount an individual is eligible to borrow. This is not a guaranty of a loan.

Premium: an amount paid on a regular schedule by a policyholder that maintains insurance coverage.

Prepayment: payment of the mortgage loan before the scheduled due date; may be Subject to a prepayment penalty.

Prepayment Penalty: a fee charged to a homeowner who pays one or more monthly payments before the due date. It can also apply to principal reduction payments.

Prepayment Penalty Mortgage (PPM): a type of mortgage that requires the borrower to pay a penalty for prepayment, partial payment of principal or for repaying the entire loan within a certain time period.

A partial payment is generally defined as an amount exceeding 20% of the original principal balance.

Price Range: the high and low amount a buyer is willing to pay for a home.

Prime Rate: the interest rate that banks charge to preferred customers. Changes in the prime rate are publicized in the business media. Prime rate can be used as the basis for adjustable rate mortgages (ARMs) or home equity lines of credit. The prime rate also affects the current interest rates being offered at a particular point in time on fixed mortgages. Changes in the prime rate do not affect the interest on a fixed mortgage.

Principal: the amount of money borrowed to buy a house or the amount of the loan that has not been paid back to the lender. This does not include the interest paid to borrow that money. The principal balance is the amount owed on a loan at any given time. It is the original loan amount minus the total repayments of principal made.

Principal, Interest, Taxes, and Insurance (PITI): the four elements of a monthly mortgage payment; payments of principal and interest go directly towards repaying the loan while the portion that covers taxes and insurance (homeowner's and mortgage, if applicable) goes into an escrow account to cover the fees when they are due.

Private Mortgage Insurance (PMI): insurance purchased by a buyer to protect the lender in the event of default. The cost of mortgage insurance is usually added to the monthly payment. Mortgage insurance is generally maintained until over 20 Percent of the outstanding amount of the loan is paid or for a set period of time, seven years is normal. Mortgage insurance may be available through a government agency, such as the Federal Housing Administration (FHA) or the Veterans Administration (VA), or through private mortgage insurance companies (PMI).

Promissory Note: a written promise to repay a specified amount over a specified period of time.

Property (Fixture and Non-Fixture): in a real estate contract, the property is the land within the legally described boundaries and all permanent structures and fixtures. Ownership of the property confers the legal right to use the property as allowed within the law and within the restrictions of zoning or easements. Fixture property refers to those items permanently attached to the structure, such as carpeting or a ceiling fan, which transfers with the property.

Property Tax: a tax charged by local government and used to fund municipal services such as schools, police, or street maintenance. The amount of property tax is determined locally by a formula, usually based on a percent per $1,000 of assessed value of the property.

Property Tax Deduction: the U.S. tax code allows homeowners to deduct the amount they have paid in property taxes from there total income.

Public Record Information: Court records of events that are a matter of public interest such as credit, bankruptcy, foreclosure and tax liens. The presence of public record information on a credit report is regarded negatively by creditors.

Punch List: a list of items that have not been completed at the time of the final walk through of a newly constructed home.

Purchase Offer: A detailed, written document that makes an offer to purchase a property, and that may be amended several times in the process of negotiations. When signed by all parties involved in the sale, the purchase offer becomes a legally binding contract, sometimes called the Sales Contract.

Q

Qualifying Ratios: guidelines utilized by lenders to determine how much money a homebuyer is qualified to borrow. Lending guidelines typically include a maximum housing expense to income ratio and a maximum monthly expense to income ratio.

Quitclaim Deed: a deed transferring ownership of a property but does not make any guarantee of clear title.

R

RESPA: Real Estate Settlement Procedures Act; a law protecting consumers from abuses during the residential real estate purchase and loan process by requiring lenders to disclose all settlement costs, practices, and relationships

Radon: a radioactive gas found in some homes that, if occurring in strong enough concentrations, can cause health problems.

Rate Cap: a limit on an ARM on how much the interest rate or mortgage payment may change. Rate caps limit how much the interest rates can rise or fall on the adjustment dates and over the life of the loan.

Rate Lock: a commitment by a lender to a borrower guaranteeing a specific interest rate over a period of time at a set cost.

Small Sacrifice, Huge Harvest

Real Estate Agent: an individual who is licensed to negotiate and arrange real estate sales; works for a real estate broker.

Real Estate Mortgage Investment Conduit (REMIC): a security representing an interest in a trust having multiple classes of securities. The securities of each class entitle investors to cash payments structured differently from the payments on the underlying mortgages.

Real Estate Property Tax Deduction: a tax deductible expense reducing a taxpayer's taxable income.

Real Estate Settlement Procedures Act (RESPA): a law protecting consumers from abuses during the residential real estate purchase and loan process by requiring lenders to disclose all settlement costs, practices, and relationships

Real Property: land, including all the natural resources and permanent buildings on it.

REALTOR?: a real estate agent or broker who is a member of the NATIONAL ASSOCIATION OF REALTORS, and its local and state associations. Recorder: the public official who keeps records of transactions concerning real property. Sometimes known as a "Registrar of Deeds" or "County Clerk."

Recording: the recording in a registrar's office of an executed legal document. These include deeds, mortgages, satisfaction of a mortgage, or an extension of a mortgage making it a part of the public record.

Recording Fees: charges for recording a deed with the appropriate government agency.

Refinancing: paying off one loan by obtaining another; refinancing is generally done to secure better loan terms (like a lower interest rate).

Rehabilitation Mortgage: a mortgage that covers the costs of rehabilitating (repairing or Improving) a property; some rehabilitation mortgages - like the FHA's 203(k) - allow a borrower to roll the costs of rehabilitation and home purchase into one mortgage loan.

Reinstatement Period: a phase of the foreclosure process where the homeowner has an opportunity to stop the foreclosure by paying money that is owed to the lender.

Remaining Balance: the amount of principal that has not yet been repaid.

Remaining Term: the original amortization term minus the number of payments that have been applied.

Repayment plan: an agreement between a lender and a delinquent borrower where the borrower agrees to make additional payments to pay down past due amounts while making regularly scheduled payments.

Return On Average Common Equity: net income available to common stockholders, as a percentage of average common stockholder equity.

Reverse Mortgage (HECM): the reverse mortgage is used by senior homeowners age 62 and older to convert the equity in their home into monthly streams of income and/or a line of credit to be repaid when they no longer occupy the home. A lending institution such as a mortgage lender, bank, credit union or savings and loan association funds the FHA insured loan, commonly known as HECM.

Right of First Refusal: a provision in an agreement that requires the owner of a property to give one party an opportunity to purchase or lease a property before it is offered for sale or lease to others.

Risk Based Capital: an amount of capital needed to offset losses during a ten-year period with adverse circumstances.

Risk Based Pricing: Fee structure used by creditors based on risks of granting credit to a borrower with a poor credit history.

Risk Scoring: an automated way to analyze a credit report verses a manual review. It takes into account late payments, outstanding debt, credit experience, and number of inquiries in an unbiased manner.

S

Sale Leaseback: when a seller deeds property to a buyer for a payment, and the buyer simultaneously leases the property back to the seller.

Second Mortgage: an additional mortgage on property. In case of a default the first mortgage must be paid before the second mortgage. Second loans are more risky for the lender and usually carry a higher interest rate.

Secondary Mortgage Market: the buying and selling of mortgage loans. Investors purchase residential mortgages originated by lenders, which in turn provides the lenders with capital for additional lending.

Secured Loan: a loan backed by collateral such as property.

Security: the property that will be pledged as collateral for a loan.

Seller Take Back: an agreement where the owner of a property provides second mortgage financing. These are often combined with an assumed mortgage instead of a portion of the seller's equity.

Serious Delinquency: a mortgage that is 90 days or more past due.

Servicer: a business that collects mortgage payments from borrowers and manages the borrower's escrow accounts.

Servicing: the collection of mortgage payments from borrowers and related responsibilities of a loan servicer.

Setback: the distance between a property line and the area where building can take place. Setbacks are used to assure space between buildings and from roads for a many of purposes including drainage and utilities.

Settlement: another name for closing.

Settlement Statement: a document required by the Real Estate Settlement Procedures Act (RESPA). It is an itemized statement of services and charges relating to the closing of a property transfer. The buyer has the right to examine the settlement statement 1 day before the closing. This is called the HUD 1 Settlement Statement.

Special Forbearance: a loss mitigation option where the lender arranges a revised repayment plan for the borrower that may include a temporary reduction or suspension of monthly loan payments.

Stockholders' Equity: the sum of proceeds from the issuance of stock and retained earnings less amounts paid to repurchase common shares.

Stripped MBS (SMBS): securities created by "stripping" or separating the principal and interest payments from the underlying pool of mortgages into two classes of securities, with each receiving a different proportion of the principal and interest payments.

Sub-Prime Loan: "B" Loan or "B" paper with FICO scores from 620 - 659. "C" Loan or "C" Paper with FICO scores typically from 580 to 619. An industry term to used to describe loans with less stringent lending and underwriting terms and conditions. Due to the higher risk, sub-prime loans charge higher interest rates and fees.

Subordinate: to place in a rank of lesser importance or to make one claim secondary to another.

Survey: a property diagram that indicates legal boundaries, easements, encroachments, rights of way, improvement locations, etc. Surveys are conducted by licensed surveyors and are normally required by the lender in order to confirm that the property boundaries and features such as buildings, and easements are correctly described in the legal description of the property.

Sweat Equity: using labor to build or improve a property as part of the down payment

T

Third Party Origination: a process by which a lender uses another party to completely or partially originate, process, underwrite, close, fund, or package the mortgages it plans to deliver to the secondary mortgage market.

Terms: The period of time and the interest rate agreed upon by the lender and the borrower to repay a loan.

Title: a legal document establishing the right of ownership and is recorded to make it part of the public record. Also known as a Deed.

Title 1: an FHA-insured loan that allows a borrower to make non-luxury improvements (like renovations or repairs) to their home; Title I loans less than $7,500 don't require a property lien.

Title Company: a company that specializes in examining and insuring titles to real estate.

Title Defect: an outstanding claim on a property that limits the ability to sell the property. Also referred to as a cloud on the title.

Title Insurance: insurance that protects the lender against any claims that arise from arguments about ownership of the property; also available for homebuyers. An insurance policy guaranteeing the accuracy of a title search protecting against errors. Most lenders require the buyer to purchase title insurance protecting the lender against loss in the event of a title defect. This charge is included in the closing costs. A policy that protects the buyer from title defects is known as an owner's policy and requires an additional charge.

Title Search: a check of public records to be sure that the seller is the recognized owner of the real estate and that there are no unsettled liens or other claims against the property.

Transfer Agent: a bank or trust company charged with keeping a record of a company's stockholders and canceling and issuing certificates as shares are bought and sold.

Transfer of Ownership: any means by which ownership of a property changes hands. These include purchase of a property, assumption of mortgage debt, exchange of possession of a property via a land sales contract or any other land trust device.

Transfer Taxes: State and local taxes charged for the transfer of real estate. Usually equal to a percentage of the sales price.

Treasury Index: can be used as the basis for adjustable rate mortgages (ARMs) It is based on the results of auctions that the U.S. Treasury holds for its Treasury bills and securities.

Truth-in-Lending: a federal law obligating a lender to give full written disclosure of all fees, terms, and conditions associated with the loan initial period and then adjusts to another rate that lasts for the term of the loan.

Two Step Mortgage: an adjustable-rate mortgage (ARM) that has one interest rate for the first five to seven years of its term and a different interest rate for the remainder of the term.

Trustee: a person who holds or controls property for the benefit of another.

U

Underwriting: the process of analyzing a loan application to determine the amount of risk involved in making the loan; it includes a review of the potential borrower's credit history and a judgment of the property value.

Up Front Charges: the fees charged to homeowners by the lender at the time of closing a mortgage loan. This includes points, broker's fees, insurance, and other charges.

V

VA (Department of Veterans Affairs): a federal agency, which guarantees loans made to veterans; similar to mortgage insurance, a loan guarantee protects lenders against loss that may result from a borrower default.

VA Mortgage: a mortgage guaranteed by the Department of Veterans Affairs (VA).

Variable Expenses: Costs or payments that may vary from month to month, for example, gasoline or food.

Variance: a special exemption of a zoning law to allow the property to be used in a manner different from an existing law.

Vested: a point in time when you may withdraw funds from an investment account, such as a retirement account, without penalty.

W

Walk Through: the final inspection of a property being sold by the buyer to confirm that any contingencies specified in the purchase agreement such as repairs have been completed, fixture and non-fixture property is in place and confirm the electrical, mechanical, and plumbing systems are in working order.

Warranty Deed: a legal document that includes the guarantee the seller is the true owner of the property, has the right to sell the property and there are no claims against the property.

Z

Zoning: local laws established to control the uses of land within a particular area. Zoning laws are used to separate residential land from areas of non-residential use, such as industry or businesses. Zoning ordinances include many provisions governing such things as type of structure, setbacks, lot size, and uses of a building.

Professional Acknowledgements

The insight given to you in this book are Small Sacrifices that you can make to get you on the right track with your finances. You'll be surprised to see the Huge Harvest of returns that await your finances once you make a few simple changes.

The Contents have been compiled from a collaboration of my personal life experiences, a host of client situations, the libraries of Equifax, Experian, and Trans-Union, The Glossaries of The Consumer Federation of America, Fair Isaac, The Department of Housing and Urban Development, Realtor Magazine, various versions of the Holy Bible, and Quotes from local Consumer Advisors.

Personal Acknowledgments

As I remember locking myself away for hours at a time, with only my laptop and a cup of tea, I must acknowledge the patience of both my husband (Lester Smith) and son (Najwa Smith) for allowing me to do so with neither complaint nor interruption. It didn't go un-noticed. Here's to my favorites, Les and Naj: "Your hugs and kisses are priceless. You make it so easy to love you both."

I will forever be grateful to my parents, (Horace and Joan Taylor) for their support and confidence in my ability to complete such a project. I guess some things never change. "Thank you so much Mom and Dad."

A special "thumbs up" to the Ladies of Reader's Digress. Although they had no knowledge of this project, each of them unknowingly encouraged me to complete this task. "I'm inspired by each one of you. It helps to be surrounded by ambitious women. Thanks for being unique both as a group and as individuals."

I reserve a special appreciation for my brother (Anthony) whose stamp of approval goes a long way with me. "Everyone should have a brother like you."

Without Family Insight, Supportive Friends, and Trusting Clients, this journey would have been a lonely one. "I'm humbled ... Truly."

To God, be the Glory for the focus to see it through to the finish.

www.ingramcontent.com/pod-product-compliance
Lightning Source LLC
Chambersburg PA
CBHW030811180526
45163CB00003B/1231